P9-APY-858

Possessing Truth in Balance

&

Anatomy of a Backslider

Victor Bentley

Possessing Truth in Balance and Anatomy of a Backslider

Victor Bentley

©1989 Word Aflame Press
Hazelwood, MO 63042-2299

Cover Design by Tim Agnew

All Scripture quotations in this book are from the King James Version of the Bible unless otherwise identified. Some verses of Scripture from the New King James Version. Copyright 1979, 1980, 1982, Thomas Nelson Inc., Publishers.

All rights reserved. No portion of this publication may be reproduced, stored in an electronic system, or transmitted in any form or by any means, electronic, mechanical, photocopy, recording, or otherwise, without the prior permission of Word Aflame Press. Brief quotations may be used in literary reviews.

Printed in United States of America.

Printed by

Bentley, Victor.

    Possessing truth in balance; and, Anatomy of a backslider / Victor Bentley.

    p. cm.

    ISBN 0-932581-48-X :
    1. Christian life—Pentecostal authors. I. Bentley, Victor. Anatomy of a backslider. 1989. II. Title. III. Title: Possessing truth in balance. IV. Title: Anatomy of a backslider.

BV4501.2.B396   1989   89-8945
248.4'8994—dc20   CIP

Possessing Truth in Balance

&

Anatomy of a Backslider

Dedication:
To Donna Bentley, my wife and best friend.

Contents

Part One

Possessing
Truth
in
Balance

1

The Narrow Way

The words of Jesus in Matthew 7:13-14 contradict the live-and-let-live, laissez-faire attitude common to much of modern religious thinking. It would be wise for all who live in these confusing times to consider these words of Jesus:

Enter ye in at the strait gate: for wide is the gate, and broad is the way, that leadeth to destruction, and many there be which go in therein; because strait is the gate, and narrow is the way, which leadeth unto life, and few there be that find it.

My ministerial travels have taken me on occasion to some very narrow roads that thread their way through the rugged hills of eastern Kentucky. Imagine the terror this city boy felt, accustomed as I was to four-lane highways, when I began navigating the extremely narrow, winding roads common throughout the Appalachian Mountains! On my right was a two-hundred-foot drop into oblivion. To my left just a few feet was a deep ditch and a rugged mountainside.

The thought of careening into a ditch and smashing into the side of a mountain held no more appeal to me than a two-hundred-foot free fall. Since my safety depended on avoiding the pitfalls that lay on both sides of the road I was travelling, I strove with great fervor to travel the straight and narrow.

The theological parallel to this Kentucky object lesson seems quite plain in the light of Matthew 7:13-14. Truth is a straight and narrow path that has pitfalls lying to either side. Unfortunately, human nature tends towards extremism and finds it difficult to stay on the straight and narrow.

For example, Jesus warned His disciples in Matthew 16:11 to beware both the leaven of the Pharisees and of the Sadducees. The Pharisees were the theological conservatives of their day and were known for their rigid observance of the law and religious custom. The Sadducees liberally interpreted the Scripture and adopted Greek culture and thinking. Jesus said to beware of both extremes.

In spite of these warnings of Jesus, many people feel that it is necessary to embrace one extreme in order to avoid the other. The presence of the Sadducees drove the Pharisees to great extremes of legalism in order to compensate for the other's liberal extremes. Today, many people have overreacted to the rigidity and pharisaical behavior of a few and have embraced the opposite extreme of liberalism and worldliness.

The history of heresy has been for the most part the history of one group's overreaction against the false teaching of another group. Arianism, embraced in its modern manifestation by the Jehovah's Witnesses, can be seen as a reaction against the trinitarian doctrine. Because the doctrine of the trinity weakened the absolute oneness of God, the Arian doctrine attempted to restore the unity of the Godhead by reducing Jesus to the status of a demigod. Thus one false teaching, which violates the oneness of God, creates another one, which robs Jesus Christ of His full majesty and deity.

Examples of the capacity of error to inspire error also exist in secular history. Many idealistic young men and women around the world turned to communism as a reaction to the fascist regimes of Francisco Franco, Benito Mussolini, and Adolf Hitler. The obvious evil of fascism caused many to embrace an equally evil movement on the opposite end of the political spectrum.

Narrow is the way that leads to life. If we will walk along the path that Jesus told us about, we will avoid the extremes that so often result in spiritual destruction. We can know the truth and ignore the siren call of extremism that beckons to us from both sides of the issues of life.

This book attempts to present a balanced perspective on various issues that affect the concerned, honest Christian—both minister and lay member. Must one decide between faith and works? Holiness and outreach? Spirit and truth? Submission and liberty? Doctrine and love? In each of the cases just cited, the answer is no. Both concepts are aspects of the truth. We can and should possess both, and thereby enjoy a balanced Christian life.

Though these and other issues have polarized the thinking of people, the Word of God can and will guide us to that "narrow way" that leads to life. We as Christians can reject the leaven of the Sadducees without running to embrace the leaven of the Pharisees. We can discover the blessing of possessing the truth in balance.

2

Revival: Producer of Perfection
versus
Result of Perfection

It is Sunday night service again at the Sackcloth and Ashes Apostolic Church. The altar is filled with weeping and wailing men and women contritely repenting over their wretched condition. Pastor Penitent eyes the moving scene with approval. It would sure be nice if there were sinners at the altar too, Pastor Penitent muses. He is somewhat annoyed that there rarely is a sinner in the service, much less at the altar. Yet Pastor Penitent fervently believes that if he can just get the church perfected a spontaneous revival will break out in which countless numbers of sinners will come and be saved. Thus, almost every sermon and Bible study is directed at correcting what Pastor Penitent feels are glaring deficiencies in the saints of his church.

Meanwhile, several decisions are being made by the weeping saints of Sackcloth and Ashes Apostolic. Bill was

15

going to witness to some friends at work, but now he feels unworthy to share the gospel. He will, instead, try to perfect himself first. Jane had been praying for her unsaved husband and family. She now feels she had best concentrate on praying for herself. She is gripped with a fear that in the end God will reject her. Tom begs God not to turn His face from him. He is almost afraid to worship God. After all, hadn't Pastor Penitent preached on God hating worship from those not willing to live the life? Tom has no deliberate sin in his life, yet he knows he could and should pray more. Ed decides to give up altogether. It will be his last service.

That same Sunday night, the Revival Time Apostolic Church is having a service also. Its altars are packed with weeping men and women, only in this case, they are mostly sinners touching God in repentance. Meanwhile other people are speaking in other tongues as they are baptized with the Holy Ghost.

Various members of Revival Time Apostolic decide to reconsecrate their lives as a result of the service. Ray determines that he is going to witness as never before. Sue vows to God that she will draw closer to Him than she ever has before. Linda dearly wants to see her family find God, and she plans to involve herself more deeply in intercessory prayer.

Does revival come as a result of a church's perfection or does revival help stimulate people toward perfection? By revival, we mean an atmosphere in which sinners are being witnessed to, are coming to church, and are finding salvation.

Let us examine the church in its infancy. Acts 2:46-47 describes the activities of the newly established body of believers: "And they, continuing daily with one accord in the temple, and breaking bread from house to house, did eat their meat with gladness and singleness of heart, praising God, and having favour with all the people. And the Lord added to the church daily such as should be saved."

The original apostolic church immediately began to reach out beyond itself and see souls saved. Jesus promised them, "Ye shall receive power, after that the Holy Ghost is come upon you: and ye shall be witnesses" (Acts 1:8). Peter and the rest of the apostles did not shut down the evangelistic arm of the church until they had all of the saints perfected. The church continued in a revival atmosphere.

The fact is, none of the apostles themselves were perfect. As great as the apostle Paul was, he did not count himself as "having apprehended." He knew perfection was a never-ending process of pressing toward the mark, yet he continued to labor for the Lord in the meantime. (See Philippians 3:12-14.)

Of course, we cannot expect God to move among a totally careless and indifferent people. The classic formula for revival preparation is found in II Chronicles 7:14: "If my people, which are called by my name, shall humble themselves, and pray, and seek my face, and turn from their wicked ways; then will I hear from heaven, and will forgive their sin, and will heal their land."

God's people must first humble themselves. "God resisteth the proud, but giveth grace unto the humble" (James 4:6). We need look no farther than the description of the Laodicean church in Revelation to see the danger of pride and feelings of self-sufficiency.

Second, they are to pray. The early church was a praying church. The Book of Acts says more about prayer than about miracles. A praying church will see people saved.

Third, God's people are to seek His face. James 4:2 says, "Ye have not, because ye ask not." The Lord promises, "Ye shall seek me, and find me, when ye shall search for me with all your heart" (Jeremiah 29:13).

Finally, God's people must turn from their wicked ways. Obviously, God cannot move as He would like to if a church is filled with people who are involved in wickedness and sin. Willful sin must be repented of—confessed and forsaken.

All of the above steps are good and necessary for a church that wants to see God save the lost. A person does not have to wait until he is perfect, however, before he can witness to a lost individual and pray for them. A church should not wait for some far-off magical moment when every single condition is ideal before it seeks out the lost through witnessing and intercessory prayer.

Amazingly, many personality conflicts and imperfections have a way of taking care of themselves when there is a revival atmosphere. It is a wonderful thing when people quit worrying about themselves all of the time and start manifesting concern for the lost around them.

Jesus told His disciples that He would make them fishers of men. Fishing consists of catching fish and cleaning them, catching fish and cleaning them, catching fish and cleaning them: a continual process. So it should be in the Lord's work. Cleaning up the lives of people and helping them to mature in Christ is important. Yet if we are to be fishers of men we must put out our evangelistic nets also. Some become so obsessed with perfection that the nets stay in the boats. Then again, some have been guilty of putting full emphasis on evangelism with little or no emphasis on teaching. Thus they catch plenty of fish but they cannot keep them or clean them.

Is preparation for revival important? Of course it is. At the same time, it is far easier for people in a revival atmosphere to aspire to deeper depths and higher heights than it is for those caught in the throes of self-condemnation and guilt.

It is important not to be like a certain young man who entered college with a determination to be a success. He was so determined to be successful that he bought every book available on the subject of how to study. His first semester he faithfully read every one of the books he had purchased. At the end of the semester he received failing grades in every course he took. The reason for his failure was that he spent so much time learning how to study that he had no time left to study.

Is revival a product of church perfection? It *is* a product of preparation, but not necessarily perfection in the ultimate sense. Revival, however, greatly helps to create an atmosphere in which people can attain maturity and aspire to perfection.

God has already given the church the tools it needs to win the lost. Those tools are the Holy Spirit and the Word of God. We do not need to wait for a perfect future to go out and win the lost. We must go now, realizing that God will go with us and will perfect us as we go.

3

Faith
versus
Works

"For by grace are ye saved through faith; and that not of yourselves: it is the gift of God: not of works, lest any man should boast" (Ephesians 2:8-9). With their feet planted firmly upon this and other like passages of Scripture, many young believers in Christ today take issue with any standards of righteousness and holiness. "We are saved by grace," they say, and on that basis they reject as totally unnecessary many holiness standards, such as men having short hair, women having long (uncut) hair, and people not going to the movies, wearing makeup, or wearing clothing that pertains to the opposite sex.

Opponents of this view sometimes respond with a verse of Scripture of their own: "But wilt thou know, O vain man, that faith without works is dead?" (James 2:20). They heartily affirm the scriptural necessity of holiness in both dress and conduct. Some of them, however, alarmed and disturbed by liberalism, begin to over-emphasize works and man's part in salvation.

One of the results of this conservative backlash is spiritual pride or Phariseeism. Testimony services with this atmosphere become bragging sessions: "Look how holy and wonderful I am—bless God, I'm glad I don't dress and act like those rotten sinners."

Sadly, they begin to resemble more and more the Pharisee who went into the Temple and prayed, "God, I thank thee, that I am not as other men are, extortioners, unjust, adulterers, or even as this publican. I fast twice in the week, I give tithes of all that I possess" (Luke 18:11-12). The poor visitor who drops in on one of these grueling sessions of self-aggrandizement will be fortunate to hear anything at all about Jesus the Savior.

The second tragic result of an overemphasis on works is the tremendous load of guilt some carry. Without full faith in Jesus Christ and the efficacy of His cleansing blood, these people never really experience the joy of salvation. They feel that they never fully measure up to God's demands and thus have no peace. Even though they do everything in their power to live righteously before God, they live in mortal terror that God will in the end reject them. Such a grim atmosphere does not promote evangelism; thus these people fail as soulwinners.

The alternative offered by the liberal "grace only" position is no less tragic. Because they feel that it does not really matter what the individual does, they possess no real motivation to forsake the ways of sin. Their "freedom" becomes in a sense a subtle form of bondage. Living like the world, dressing like the world, and talking like the world, they have little light to shine for the man or woman looking to be set free from the world.

Faith versus works where is the straight and narrow path that cuts between these positions? Does the Word of God provide an alternative to the pride of Phariseeism or the carnal rejection of scriptural standards of righteousness?

Yes, there is an alternative, and it is found through a clear understanding of what the Scriptures, including both Ephesians and James, actually teach concerning faith and works. We must remember, first of all, that both Paul and James were moved upon by the Holy Ghost as they composed their respective epistles. God, who is not the author of confusion, never intended for the Books of James and Ephesians to contradict each other. In fact, careful study of the works of Paul and James will show a harmony in their teaching.

First of all, let us consider Paul's teaching on the subject of grace. There is no question that we are saved by grace through faith in Jesus Christ. Without the shed blood of Jesus Christ at Calvary, without His divine mercy, without His calling us out of sin and darkness, we could never have been saved.

No amount of good works could ever have earned our salvation. "But we are all as an unclean thing, and all our righteousnesses are as filthy rags" (Isaiah 64:6). If every woman in America would refrain from cutting her hair and wearing immodest and masculine apparel, and if every individual in America threw away his drugs, alcohol, and cigarettes and quit living immorally, they would still be lost without Jesus Christ.

The cold, hard facts are that Christ died for the ungodly. We were wretched sinners when God began to woo us with His love. Our testimony is not how wonderful and holy we are, but "love lifted me." "Amazing grace, how sweet the sound, that saved a wretch like me! I once was lost but now am found, was blind but now I see." This message is what Paul conveyed to the believers in Ephesus when he said, "Not of works." In other words, without the love that sent Jesus Christ to die at Calvary we would all be lost, regardless of how we would have lived. Righteousness or works is not the prerequisite of salvation; we are indeed saved by grace.

Salvation by grace is not a license for loose living, however. After explaining the doctrine of justification by faith in Christ, Paul asked, "What shall we say then? Shall we continue in sin that grace may abound?" (Romans 6:1). His answer was, "God forbid. How shall we, that are dead to sin, live any longer therein?" (Romans 6:2).

Paul further explained in Romans 6 that as we once yielded ourselves as servants of unrighteousness, we should now give ourselves to be servants of righteousness. When we obeyed the lustful desires of our flesh we were servants to sin. Now that we have been saved, we have been freed from serving sin in order for us to serve righteousness. Verse 16 says we become servants of whatever master we choose—either sin unto death or obedience unto righteousness.

Thus righteousness (or works), though it is not a prerequisite for salvation, will be a product of the salvation experience. We are not saved because we are righteous, but we are righteous because we are saved. We are God's workmanship, "created in Christ Jesus unto good works, which God hath before ordained that we should walk in them" (Ephesians 2:10). True faith includes obedience and is shown by good works. "Shew me thy faith without thy works, and I will shew thee my faith by my works" (James 2:18).

James did not dispute the fact that we are saved by grace through faith, but he contended that faith is more than an abstract intellectual assent; rather, it is a powerful force that will manifest itself in our lives by motivating us to good works.

In writing to Titus concerning the grace of God, Paul revealed that not only does grace save us but it also teaches us: "For the grace of God that bringeth salvation hath appeared to all men, teaching us that, denying ungodliness and worldly lusts, we should live soberly, righteously, and godly, in this present world" (Titus 2:11-12).

Salvation does and should change a person. Christ died to reconcile the sinner, not the sin. His blood does not excuse unrighteousness and make sin acceptable to God; it washes away unrighteousness and makes the sinner acceptable to God. The Cross does not lower God's standard of acceptance; rather, it lifts a person to meet that standard by justifying and then progressively transforming him.

A Christian should reject the boasting and pride of Phariseeism. We are all sinners saved by grace; we cannot boast of ourselves. Any good thing in us is due to the power of Christ that works within us. Yet the debt of love we owe Him will motivate us to seek after holiness and righteousness.

Yes, our lives should be filled with good works. We should not try to do good works in order to exalt self but rather to exalt Christ. While the church must set aside pride and spiritual Phariseeism it should not abandon the standards that the Word of God teaches. Must we choose between faith and works? No, faith and works go hand in hand. Works without faith are of no spiritual value, and faith without works is not genuine faith. As we have both faith and works, we will show the world what Jesus has wrought in our lives by His grace.

4

Holiness
versus
Outreach

The Dynamic Evangelistic Center, formerly the Sometown Apostolic Church, is exploding with growth at an unbelievable pace. Led by a dynamic pastor and an efficient and dedicated staff, the church is geared for high-powered evangelism. The services themselves are ideal patterns of carefully orchestrated worship, music, and preaching. There are no rough edges here!

In the midst of this well-oiled and maintained evangelistic mechanism sits Sammy Sincere. Sammy, like most of the people who lived through the evolution of Sometown Apostolic Church to the Dynamic Evangelistic Center, is thrilled by the effective outreach of his assembly into the community. Sammy also admires his pastor's obvious dedication to growth.

Yet Sammy is not happy. Quite simply, he cannot understand the sudden de-emphasis of practical holiness in what at one time was a holiness-believing assembly. The long hair of some of the men and the makeup and cut hair of some of the women send him into shock. The former pastors of his assembly had taught against these practices as being contrary to God's Word. Seeing some of the young ladies in the congregation begin to wear pants proves to be the proverbial last straw.

"Pastor, what has happened to our holiness standards?" asks Sammy in a contrite but firm manner.

"Come on, Sammy, let's not worry about such trivial matters as hair, pants, movies, and other traditional taboos. We've got a world to win!" The pastor smiles condescendingly at "poor ignorant Sammy." He would like to instruct Sammy more on progressive outreach, but his wrist alarm beeps a reminder of his next appointment. "Remember, Sammy," the pastor calls out as he rushes to his next appointment, "outreach is our number-one concern at Dynamic Evangelistic Center."

The next Sunday, Sammy sincere visits the Hardline Holiness Apostolic Church. What a refreshing change! The men, all four of them, are clean cut and the ladies look as apostolic ladies should look. Sammy smiles as he hears testimony after testimony about how "we're gonna hold the line around here; we ain't gonna give in."

The sermon is entitled "An Encyclopedia of Sinful Practices," and sure enough, Brother Hardshell preaches for over two hours against sins ranging from alcoholism to Zen Buddhism and everything in between. Since there are no visitors other than Sammy, there is no evangelistic appeal, only an altar call for the hypocrite, the compromiser, and the jellyfish present among the crowd of eight.

After weeping at the altar, Sammy informs Brother Hardshell that he wants to start coming to Hardline Apostolic. Sammy tells him he always wanted to help in a home mission church.

"What do you mean home mission work!" the pastor exclaims in an insulted manner. "I've been here for thirty years."

Sammy, somewhat embarrassed, tries to salvage himself. "I'm sorry, Brother Hardshell, I wasn't trying to insult you. I just want to go to church somewhere where holiness is taught and preached. Why, I would love to help out with your outreach. That is, after I secure a letter from my pastor and prove myself here at Hardline."

Brother Hardshell snorts in derision. "You don't need no letter to go here, but you can forget this outreach stuff. As far as I'm concerned it's a trick of the devil. Ain't nobody wanting to live for God anyway, except us chosen few. I say a crowd condemns holiness people. We're running fifteen in Sunday school now, and that's already too big. It's time to run off a few devils."

Sammy notices that Brother Hardshell is staring disgustedly at his watchband. "If you go to church here, you'll have to walk the chalk, and that means all worldliness has to go." Again, Brother Hardshell stares at Sammy's watchband.

Sammy is now in a dilemma. He can go to a church that is reaching out for souls but has sacrificed many scriptural standards of holiness, or he can change to a church that preaches and teaches outward holiness but manifests no real concern to reach the lost.

Outreach versus holiness—which is most important? Is compromise necessary or desirable to bring about growth? Must holiness bring about isolation from humanity and inhibit growth?

There is no doubt that both outreach and holiness are desirable and necessary goals for a church. Unfortunately some churches that emphasize growth, outreach, and evangelism do so at the exclusion of teaching righteousness and holy living. On the other hand, some who stress holiness and righteous living do so at the expense or exclusion of evangelism and outreach.

The answer to Sammy's dilemma lies in a balanced biblical perspective on these two important subjects. Let us consider outreach first of all.

The command of Jesus in Mark 16:15 leaves no doubt that He meant for outreach to have a high priority in the apostolic church: "And he said unto them, Go ye into all the world, and preach the gospel to every creature." In fact, the Holy Ghost was poured out upon the church for the purpose of evangelism. "But ye shall receive power, after that the Holy Ghost is come upon you: and ye shall be witnesses unto me both in Jerusalem, and in all Judaea, and in Samaria, and unto the uttermost part of the earth" (Acts 1:8).

These verses of Scripture and a careful reading of the Book of Acts demonstrate that God's church is an evangelism-oriented church. In the early church, "the Lord added to the church daily such as should be saved" (Acts 2:47). We cannot imagine men such as Peter or Paul meeting in an isolated corner of Jerusalem with a handful of saints and a sign outside flashing "no vacancy."

There is no excuse for God's people not to do everything in their power to reach the lost. That is our commission. To fold our arms and use holiness as an excuse for thinking small, acting small, and not caring for the lost is a tragic disregard of apostolic purpose. No church valued outreach and soulwinning more than the first-century Christian church.

Yet outreach was not the only priority in the early church. Paul wrote to the Corinthians concerning another essential issue: "Wherefore, come out from among them and be ye separate, saith the Lord, and touch not the unclean thing; and I will receive you, and will be a Father unto you, and ye shall be my sons and daughters, saith the Lord Almighty. Having therefore these promises, dearly beloved, let us cleanse ourselves from all filthiness of the flesh and spirit, perfecting holiness in the fear of God" (II Corinthians 6:17-7:1).

Just as we cannot imagine Peter or Paul pastoring an isolated group of saints unconcerned for the lost, it is just as hard to imagine either one of them leading a worldly, anything-goes congregation devoid of real holiness. Peter recorded the command of God: "Be ye holy; for I am holy" (I Peter 1:16).

Those who advocate outreach to the exclusion of everything else might well consider the words of Psalm 127:1: "Except the LORD build the house, they labour in vain that build it." Of what value is it to bring in masses by Madison Avenue tactics coupled with managerial excellence and then not lead them to the Acts 2:38 experience and also teach them how to forsake worldly desires? Has God not always desired a separated people?

Were size and rapidity of growth the only criteria for the church, then we might well join the Mormon church, the Catholic church, or any large or quickly growing organization. God, who is not willing that any should

31

perish, does desire quantity, but not at the expense of quality.

Yet let it also be said that quality does not have to exclude quantity. It is foolish indeed to assume that every church that experiences growth does so by compromise.

Pity poor Sammy Sincere. It is too bad he is forced to choose between growth and perfection, between holiness and outreach. God can temper charisma with conviction and conviction with love. Sammy's only hope is that the pastor of Dynamic Evangelistic Center will consider again the old paths of holiness and righteousness and have the courage to reverse the trends towards worldliness, or that Brother Hardshell will repent of his Phariseeism and be baptized with a love for the lost. Until then, in Sammy's life it will be holiness versus outreach—a conflict that the apostles would never have understood or accepted.

The balanced church is one that actively seeks to save the lost but at the same time holds to Bible standards of holiness. Both quantity and quality are its goals.

In many ways, the balanced church must be built as Nehemiah rebuilt the walls of Jerusalem. According to Nehemiah 4, the enemies of the Jews were upset that the walls of Jerusalem were being rebuilt. Consequently, Sanballat, Tobiah, and their evil associates threatened to come out and fight against Jerusalem. Nehemiah 4:17 records the response of Nehemiah and his builders to the threat: "They which builded on the wall, and they that bare burdens, with those that laded, every one with one of his hands wrought in the work, and with the other hand held a weapon."

What a beautiful illustration of a balance between

holiness and outreach! With one hand the church reaches out to a lost world to rescue the perishing, constantly building up the work of God. Yet at the same time the other hand firmly grasps the sword of the Spirit, which is the Word of God. The gospel worker keeps a watchful eye on the enemy, making sure that while the church reaches out into the world the world does not reach into the church.

Sure, the walls could have been built faster if the Jews had used both hands to build, but that would have opened them to the power of the enemy. Even so, the church today must not neglect its defense, and holiness is its defense against the tactics of the enemy.

Then again, those intrepid men under Nehemiah did not quit building just because there was an enemy. Likewise, as the church today maintains holiness, it must not forget the lost. God hates sin, but He loves the sinner.

May God help us to find the straight path that incorporates both outreach and holiness, for God wants us to excel in both.

5

Spirit
versus
Truth

The Samaritan woman who met Jesus at Jacob's well wanted an answer to a contemporary controversy. The Samaritans worshiped in a mountain; the Jews worshiped in Jerusalem. Now just who, this woman wondered, was worshiping correctly? Where does true worship take place?

Jesus explained, "But the hour cometh, and now is, when the true worshippers shall worship the Father in spirit and in truth: for the Father seeketh such to worship him. God is a Spirit: and they that worship him must worship him in spirit and in truth" (John 4:23-24).

This answer of Jesus forever ended any argument of Jerusalem versus Samaria as a primary place of worship. True worshipers, He declared, would worship in spirit and in truth, regardless of physical location.

Now, a new controversy rages concerning the nature

of true worship. No longer is it Samaria versus Jerusalem. Now, it is spirit versus truth.

How is that? someone may wonder. Spirit *versus* truth? Didn't Jesus say spirit *and* truth? Yes, but that makes no difference to those who choose to take spirit and truth as an either/or proposition.

Let us listen now as Brother Leaper of Wildfire Apostolic declares that people should worship in spirit.

"I believe we need to worship in spirit and in spirit only. When you worship in spirit you don't need nothing else! The Lord has really blessed us here at Wildfire Apostolic. I haven't had to preach in eight months. Why interrupt old-time shouting for a sermon? In fact, I traded my Thompson Chain Bible and concordance for a pair of jogging shoes. I'm going to run and shout and leap about and forget quenching the Spirit with a Bible study."

Brother Leaper dances back to his seat as Brother Stoic strides to the podium to refute Brother Leaper. "The most important thing is truth. We need to reject all of this emotionalism and be serious students of the Word. In my church we don't have time to waste in spirited worship. Then again, I suppose after my two-hour messages they're too tired to shout. One thing for sure, I've grounded them in truth. You can keep your spirit; I'll stick with truth."

If ever a subject required a balanced perspective, it is the subject of spirit and truth in worship. As a pastor I am amazed at the number of people who seem to feel that we must choose between spirit and truth.

Why choose? It is a marvelous thing to worship God freely. When the ark of God returned to Jerusalem, David was so overjoyed that he danced before the Lord with all his might and came shouting and leaping. This he did unashamedly in the presence of all Israel. His wife rebuked him for this behavior, and she became barren as a result. If a dignified king could worship freely when the ark, which was symbolic of God's presence, returned to Jerusalem, how much more should we do the same when the literal presence of God comes in our midst!

Throughout the Book of Psalms we are instructed to lift our hands in praise (141:2), to sing and play musical instruments (33:2-3), to make a joyful noise (95:1-2), to rejoice and sing praises. No one is excluded: "Let every thing that hath breath praise the LORD. Praise ye the LORD" (Psalm 150:6).

We see no change in the importance of spirited worship in the New Testament. The 120 who received the Holy Ghost in Acts 2 rejoiced and made so much noise that a huge crowd of curiosity seekers gathered. Their worship was so exuberant that it led many of the onlookers to the false conclusion that these Spirit-filled believers were drunk. These worshipers certainly worshiped in spirit!

We must never become guilty of quenching the Spirit in our worship. If we become bound by false tradition and formalism, it is possible to program the move of God out of our services. True worshipers will worship Him in spirit.

Yet even as truth without spirit is formalism, so spirit without truth is fanaticism.

Although there are times when God will move in a service in such a way that no preaching will go forth, that is not always the desired pattern. There have been churches that have practically eliminated the preaching of the Word of God and replaced it with demonstrative worship, but this situation soon ends in tragedy.

"Faith cometh by hearing, and hearing by the word of God" (Romans 10:17). God places strong emphasis upon preaching (I Corinthians 1:18, 21). A strong church is a church in which truth is proclaimed. We need the powerful preaching of truth without fear or favor. We need Holy Ghost-inspired teachers of the Word to root us and ground us in the truth of God's Word. True worshipers will worship Him in truth.

Spirit versus truth? That is how Satan would have us to view the issue. How he would love to see a congregation go into unscriptural fanaticism and excess due to an unbalanced program of spirited worship without strong preaching and teaching of truth! Nor would he mind seeing a church become numb and cold with formalism and ritual. The letter without the spirit is dead.

God wants us to worship both in spirit and in truth. May we be a people who sing and shout and worship God, and when the singing is over, praise God for the preaching of truth from the Word of God.

When spirit and truth are both present in the worship of God's people, what a powerful combination they make! True, heartfelt worship prepares the hearts of people to receive God's Word.

For example, let us examine once again what happened on the Day of Pentecost. The 120 who were filled with the Holy Ghost worshiped so freely that many thought they were drunk. After such a tremendous pouring out of God's Spirit and blessings, they could have ended the service, shaken hands, and gone home, saying, "What a time we had!" They were not about to close, however, without proclaiming the truth of what God had done. Brother Peter took the pulpit with the general board standing behind him and preached to the onlookers who had come out to see the show. The result was that instead of 120 going home with a Holy Ghost afterglow, 3,120 went home singing, "It's real, it's real, I know it's real, this Pentecostal blessing, and I know, I know it's real."

In Acts 3, a group of people assembled together in the Temple at the hour of prayer. We can imagine how they must have felt when into their midst burst a man walking, leaping, and praising God. There was a man who had been lame from his mother's womb, and they all saw him walking and praising God. We can be sure that there was one man who was worshiping God in spirit! Peter and John must have been feeling good about that time also.

As the formerly lame man worshiped God in spirit, a large group assembled at Solomon's Porch, wondering what had happened. Brother Peter did not waste any time in combining truth with spirit as he preached about the power of the name of Jesus.

Our message as well as our worship sets us apart from the masses. The power of Pentecost is in spirit and in truth. May God give us the courage to continue in the freedom and diversity of our worship while at the same time proclaiming the truth of the Holy Ghost, water baptism, the power of Jesus' name, and the mighty God in Christ. Truth without spirit is dead formalism; spirit without truth is fanaticism.

In spirit *and* in truth is where we will always find the true worshipers.

6

Love
versus
Doctrine

I t was a classic confrontation. In the back of the church
a discussion was taking place. After a very moving service the pastor, a seasoned elder in the Lord, was sharing Scripture with a group of young visitors in their early twenties. As the pastor discussed baptism and other
instructions from the Bible, the leader of the young group
shook his head disgustedly. Finally, with a sneer, he cut
off the pastor and said loudly, "You don't love Jesus, man,
you love your doctrine. Me, I love Jesus." The group of
young visitors followed their leader as he strode angrily
out of the church.

The young man's disdain of doctrine and espousal of
love for Jesus has become quite prevalent among some
young people who have in one fashion or another "turned
on to Jesus." The ecumenical cry for unity is rever-
berating throughout the denominational world. "Tear

41

down the doctrinal walls that separate us," church members cry. "Let's just love one another and love Jesus." Priest and preacher, liberal and conservative, all seem to be echoing the sentiments of a now deceased agnostic who declared "All you need is love."

Bookstores abound with books on charismatic renewal and love. The authors gush with excitement as they describe charismatic love feasts in which Protestant preachers hug the necks of Catholic priests and profess their love and unity. Why let little things like Mariolatry, veneration of saints and statues, penance, and the pope stand in the way of loving unity? Who needs doctrine anyway?

Indeed, doctrine often becomes an object of scorn. It is considered divisive and so is avoided. The term *nondenominational* is worn as a badge of pride. The battle lines are thus drawn: love versus doctrine; doctrine versus love.

Can they possibly coexist peacefully? Must doctrine be scrapped in the name of love? More important, should it be?

The apostle Paul, writing under the inspiration of the Holy Ghost, had much to say about both love and doctrine. Perhaps his inspired words can reconcile these seemingly conflicting themes.

Paul taught that we should love God and love one another. Concerning love, no more stirring chapter has been written in the Bible than I Corinthians 13. In Romans 13:8, Paul instructed us, "Owe no man any thing, but to love one another: for he that loveth another hath fulfilled the law." In II Corinthians 11:23-28 Paul related some of the hardship he endured to preach the gospel of Christ.

There is no doubt that he loved Jesus Christ and loved people.

Yet as much as Paul preached, believed, and practiced love, he also preached doctrine. Paul desired unity in the church, but he emphasized that unity had to be based on sound doctrine: "But though we, or an angel from heaven, preach any other gospel unto you than that which we have preached unto you, let him be accursed. As we said before, so say I now again, If any man preach any other gospel unto you than that ye have received, let him be accursed" (Galatians 1:8-9).

It is evident that Paul considered what a person preached to be of utmost importance. Clearly, then, doctrine was vitally important to him. Paul instructed Timothy, "Take heed unto thyself, and unto the doctrine; continue in them: for in doing this thou shalt both save thyself, and them that hear thee" (I Timothy 4:16).

Can someone really separate loving God from loving His doctrine? What is doctrine, but the instructions of God's Word? "For this is the love of God, that we keep his commandments: and his commandments are not grievous" (I John 5:3).

A person who truly loves God will also love doctrine, for true love creates a desire for obedience in the one who loves. Solomon declared in Proverbs 13:1, "A wise son heareth his father's instruction: but a scorner heareth not rebuke." If it is important for a son to hear his earthly father's instruction, how much more important is it for the Christian to hear the doctrine (instruction) of his heavenly Father?

What about the argument that doctrine is divisive and that people who love Jesus should not allow doctrinal walls to separate them from fellowship? First of all, fellowship must be based on truth. We may have differences of opinion in some areas, but there must be agreement on the central teachings of God's Word, on the essentials of the faith. "But if we walk in the light, as he is in the light, we have fellowship one with another" (I John 1:7). Our fellowship with Jesus Christ is dependent not on just saying we love Him, but on walking in the light. There are many people who with their lips profess to love Christ but who are unwilling to walk in the light.

Should we have fellowship with groups that fail to preach truth, that do not uphold the biblical standard of holiness? (By fellowship we mean a close-knit relationship, a mutual sharing, and most of all, an approval of lifestyle.) Should every group that claims to love Jesus be automatically approved and accepted? Not if they do not walk in the light: "Be ye not unequally yoked together with unbelievers: for what fellowship hath righteousness with unrighteousness? and what communion hath light with darkness?" (II Corinthians 6:14). (See also Romans 16:17; II Thessalonians 3:14.)

We should love those who do not follow the truth of God's Word, for Christ loved us while we were yet sinners. We should in humility try to show them the way of God more perfectly. We dare not become yoked with them, however, or compromise the doctrine that God has graciously revealed to us in His Word.

It is a frustrating thing to the believer to meet people who talk about Jesus and how much they love Him and yet flatly reject sound doctrine from the Word of God. It is amazing how that some individuals will smile from ear to ear and talk endlessly about love but will almost curse and become angry when someone asks them, "Have you read in the Bible about. . . ?"

In writing to Timothy, Paul warned that this very thing would happen: "Preach the word; be instant in season, out of season; reprove, rebuke, exhort with all longsuffering and doctrine. For the time will come when they will not endure sound doctrine; but after their own lusts shall they heap to themselves teachers, having itching ears" (II Timothy 4:2-3).

In other words, there will be people who simply will not put up with straight preaching and doctrine. The reason is simple: they are too interested in pursuing their own worldly desires. Many times, people who reject doctrine and do not want a pastor or a church simply want to be free to fulfill the lusts of their flesh without interference. They will have fellowship with anybody or everybody because they have no convictions to be compromised.

Throughout the history of God's people there have been and will be people who confess God with their lips but have hearts far from Him. Jesus warned, "Not every one that saith unto me, Lord, Lord, shall enter into the kingdom of heaven; but he that doeth the will of my Father which is in heaven" (Matthew 7:21).

Love versus doctrine? No, for the person who truly loves the Lord there is no need to choose between the two. If we truly love God we will love His Word and the commandments contained in His Word (John 14:15; I John 2:5). We will love doctrine, and as the early church, we will continue "steadfastly in the apostles' doctrine and fellowship" (Acts 2:42).

7

Submission to Man
versus
Submission to God

The Word of God instructs the hearts of those who would please God, though some instructions are easier to receive than others. One of those areas of instruction that seem to run contrary to human nature is obedience and submission. *Webster's Dictionary* defines the word *submit* as "yielding to the power or control of another." There are at least four different areas in which the Scriptures teach submission to human authority.

1. "Wives, submit yourselves unto your own husbands, as unto the Lord. For the husband is the head of the wife, even as Christ is the head of the church: and he is saviour of the body" (Ephesians 5:22-23). The Lord tells wives to submit to the family leadership of their own husbands. This passage of Scripture does not place a woman under every man's authority, only that of her husband. God does not mean that a woman should have no

input into the marriage, for marriage is a partnership (I Peter 3:7), but in situations where a family decision must be made, the final authority rests with the husband. Though it may be difficult at times, God has instructed wives to respect the authority of their husbands.

Of course, husbands have the ultimate responsibility to provide for the home, and they must love their wives so much that they will consider their wives' needs and desires as much as their own (Ephesians 5:25, 28). In a broad sense, then, husbands and wives submit to each other (Ephesians 5:21).

2. "Children, obey your parents in the Lord: for this is right" (Ephesians 6:1). The Bible is quite clear on the subject of children obeying their parents. Under Old Testament law, a stubborn and rebellious child was to be taken outside of the camp and stoned to death (Deuteronomy 21:20). In recent times, however, many mothers and fathers have begun raising their children by a new book rather than the Bible. This new philosophy de-emphasizes discipline and correction of children and instructs parents to be tolerant of their child's disobedience. The results have been tragic as a generation of aimless, undisciplined, and rebellious children have grown into aimless, undisciplined, and rebellious adults.

Children need the strong leadership of parents, and it is a wise child who will submit to his parent's authority. Every individual who takes on the responsibilities of marriage and parenthood seems to look back on his own childhood and realize how wise Mom and Dad were after all.

3. "Submit yourselves to every ordinance of man for the Lord's sake: whether it be to the king, as supreme;

or unto governors, as unto them that are sent by him for the punishment of evildoers, and for the praise of them that do well" (I Peter 2:13-14). God desires His people to be law-abiding citizens. True Christians do not embezzle funds, defraud the government, or cheat on income tax. We may not always like the person who holds a particular office or his policies, but the Word of God instructs us to submit to the law. After all, God is sovereign, and just as He can allow people to rise to power, He can bring about their removal. Jesus summed it all up when He said, "Render therefore unto Caesar, the things which are Caesar's" (Matthew 22:21). That includes taxes and traffic laws—"every" ordinance of man.

4. "Obey them that have the rule over you, and submit yourselves: for they watch for your souls, as they that must give account, that they may do it with joy, and not with grief: for that is unprofitable for you" (Hebrews 13:17). God commands His people to be obedient and submit themselves to spiritual leadership. In recent years we have seen the tragedy of individuals who claim an apostolic experience but refuse to submit themselves to any authority. These spiritual tumbleweeds have no church and no pastor; they are content to drift aimlessly from place to place. Often they sit at home with an electronic "pastor" who ministers to them via radio, television, or cassette tape. Naturally these electronic "pastors" are incapable of reproving, rebuking, or exhorting their faceless flock. A person who does not have a pastor and who is unwilling to submit to spiritual authority is out of the will of God as revealed in God's written Word.

Most people who have problems obeying these scriptural teachings on submission simply do not want to be submissive in some area. Yet sometimes situations arise in which people truly want to be submissive to the authority ordained by God (whether it be husband, parent, government, or pastor), but they sincerely feel that to do so would place them in conflict with God.

Since in all of the preceding areas God has commanded submission and obedience, in a sense submission to humans in these areas is a form of submission to God. In most cases we never face the dilemma of submission to man versus submission to God. Is it possible, however, for someone to face a situation in which he would have to choose between obeying man and obeying God? Are the four areas of submission mentioned—children to parents, saints to pastor, wife to husband, and citizen to government—absolute, without exception?

Is there a scriptural answer to the wife whose husband forbids her to pray, read her Bible, or go to church? Must Christians submit to a government that passes laws against Bible ownership? What recourse do saints have if their pastor goes astray and begins to abuse his authority, live immorally, or preach false doctrine?

To find the proper response to these dilemmas, let us examine how the apostle Peter reacted in a situation in which he had to choose between obeying God and following the very principle he expounded in I Peter 2:13, that is, obeying civil government. In Acts 5, the Sanhedrin, the ruling religious body of the Jews, berated Peter and the other apostles for teaching in the name of Jesus. Acts 5:28-29 records the Sanhedrin's charge and the apostles' response: "Did not we straitly command you that ye should not teach in this name? and, behold, ye have filled Jerusalem with your doctrine, and intend to bring this man's blood upon us. Then Peter and the other apostles answered and said, We ought to obey God rather than men."

When it boiled down to obeying human authority versus God's authority, Peter did not hesitate to obey God. Likewise, the apostle Paul, who in many of his epistles emphasized submission to spiritual authority, told the Galatians, "But though we or an angel from heaven, preach any other gospel unto you than which we have preached unto you, let him be accursed" (Galatians 1:8). Paul let them know that if it came to a choice between him and the gospel he had delivered to them, they must stay with the truth. Even with respect to spiritual leaders, we ought to obey God rather than men.

It must be emphasized again, however, that it *is* God's will for a child to obey his parents, for a wife to submit to her husband, for a citizen to submit to civil authority, and for Christians to submit to spiritual leadership. Therefore, a person must be very sure that it really is a matter of obeying God rather than man when he or she decides not to act in accordance with parents, husband, government, or pastor.

In other words, a person cannot say, "I don't like the government's foreign policy so I'll just quit paying taxes." Or "I feel the Lord told me He wanted the auditorium painted green but my pastor decided on blue. Therefore, I'm going to quit going to church" (or paying tithes, or worshiping). A wife would not be justified in saying, "I want to go to the general conference, but my unsaved husband says it is too far away and we can't afford it. Therefore, I'll just slip out of the house at two a.m. with my suitcase and the charge cards and go anyway."

Many people wrongly try to excuse their rebellion by claiming they want to obey God rather than man. Yet for the sincere Christian, it is comforting to know that we are not bound to submission to any human authority to the point that we would have to disobey God.

Submission to man versus submission to God? Fortunately, most of us are usually not forced to choose between the two. But if we are, may God grant us the wisdom and courage to obey and submit to God.

8

Mourning
versus
Joyfulness

M eet Happy Henry. Henry believes fervently that "a merry heart doeth good like a medicine" (Proverbs 17:22). In fact, Henry is a veritable pharmacy when it comes to dispensing joy and laughter. He loves the fellowship of the saints and looks forward to the after-service Coke as much as to the actual service itself.

Happy Henry loves the Lord, but he gets very uncomfortable when a solemn spirit sweeps over the congregation. Henry loves shouting and singing, but weeping is definitely not in his repertoire. Whenever a church softball game or other social function is announced, Henry is there on time and eager. Yet Henry finds it almost impossible to find time to pray. The door of the prayer room is rarely darkened by Happy Henry.

No one is upset by Happy Henry more than Mournful Mike. First of all, Mike cannot understand how Henry can be so happy all the time. How dare Henry laugh and tell jokes when a world full of people is dying and going to hell? Mike worries that Henry's spirit of frivolity has corrupted the entire church. To his dismay, Mike has even seen the pastor smile and, worse yet, actually laugh behind the pulpit. Has he not read, Mike wonders, that "blessed are they that mourn?"

Mike has no trouble finding time to pray. He especially likes to go to church and pray on days the rest of the church is having a softball game, picnic, or other such "carnal" activity. He feels a rush of pride knowing he has spent eight hours in prayer while others were laughing and having fun. Mike avoids fellowship after church, not wanting to taint himself. He sees too many of his brethren giving into the devil and acquiring girlfriends. Some even go so far as to get married.

Mournful Mike can be seen wearing his long face and saddened countenance faithfully to every service. He pities the carnal people who comprise the rest of the church and often wonders why his pastor is not as spiritual as himself. Mike especially fears for the soul of Happy Henry, and he breathes a prayer to God, every so often, thanking Him that he is nothing like lighthearted Happy Henry. Yet Mournful Mike and Happy Henry share a common characteristic: both have acquired an unbalanced approach to living for God.

Mourning versus joy. Sobriety versus happiness. Happy Henry's lifestyle versus Mournful Mike's. Does the Bible offer a balance between these diametrically opposed concepts?

Let us consider the divinely inspired words of the wisest man who ever lived: "To every thing there is a season, and a time to every purpose under the heaven: a time to be born, and a time to die; a time to plant, and time to pluck up that which is planted; a time to kill, and a time to heal; a time to break down, and a time to build up; a time to weep, and a time to laugh; a time to mourn, and a time to dance" (Ecclesiastes 3:1-4).

Paul invoked Solomon's principle in his advice to the Romans: "Rejoice with them that do rejoice, and weep with them that weep" (Romans 12:15). Quite simply, there are times when it is not appropriate to laugh and be jovial, just as there are times when it is not appropriate to be mournful.

Happy Henry would do well to realize that he needs to make a place in his life for sober contemplation and bearing of burdens on behalf of others. "Blessed are they that mourn: for they shall be comforted" (Matthew 5:4). Happy Henry should be willing to open his heart to the hurts and sorrows of those around him. A stark realization of what sin does to the lives of individuals will motivate him to develop intercessory prayer in his life.

One of the richest and most joyous experiences a Christian can know is the winning of a soul. But soulwinning begins with a burden. Often the soulwinner will weep many a tear over a lost friend or loved one in intercessory prayer before there are results. He has much joy, however, when that friend or loved one comes to Christ. What a thrill a church experiences when, after a season of weeping and soul searching, revival comes, bringing with it a great harvest of souls! "They that sow in tears shall reap in joy. He that goeth forth and weepeth, bearing precious seed, shall doubtless come again with rejoicing, bringing his sheaves with him" (Psalm 126:5-6).

Henry, who loves to be happy and joyful, ends up denying himself the greatest joys by not acquainting himself with the depths of caring and mourning for the lost around him. Henry needs to discover a time for weeping.

While Henry is weeping in the prayer room, it would be wise for Mournful Mike to reexamine his life and find the joy of serving God, "for the joy of the LORD is your strength" (Nehemiah 8:10).

Humans were not made to be in a perpetual state of sorrow and mourning. Proverbs 15:13 tells us that "by sorrow of the heart the spirit is broken." Proverbs 17:22 warns us that a "broken spirit drieth the bones." Unless Mournful Mike allows a place for joy and laughter in his life, he will soon find his spiritual strength ebbing away. He will feel depressed and defeated.

Moreover, he will find that in spite of his burden and prayer, his witness will not be effective. David recognized the need of joy in one's life in order to be effective in converting sinners: "Restore unto me the joy of thy salvation; and uphold me with thy free spirit. Then will I teach transgressors thy ways; and sinners shall be converted unto thee" (Psalm 51:12-13).

It is hard to imagine how any sinner would find Mournful Mike's testimony inspiring. His life seems to say, "I used to be happy, I used to smile, I even used to enjoy myself, but then Jesus saved me from all that. Come and visit my church, and you too can have a long face and look miserable." Who would find such a life attractive and desirable?

It would be wise for both Mike and Henry to look to the perfect example of a balanced life: Jesus Christ. "And

Jesus increased in wisdom and stature, and in favour with God and man" (Luke 2:52). As the young Jesus matured, He developed mentally, physically, and socially as well as spiritually.

First of all, let us consider physical development. Some have misinterpreted the words of Paul in I Timothy 4:7-8 to mean that bodily exercise is of practically no value. A careful examination of this passage in its context, however, will reveal that such is not the case: "But refuse profane and old wives' fables, and exercise thyself rather unto godliness. For bodily exercise profiteth little: but godliness is profitable unto all things, having promise of the life that now is, and of that which is to come." The key to understanding this text is the phrase "profiteth little." It is a reference to time rather than to the overall value of bodily exercise. In essence, Paul was saying, "Timothy, your father was Greek, and you know the value the Greeks place on a sound mind and a sound body. Yet as beneficial as bodily exercise is, its benefits are limited by time. No matter how hard you exercise, you will die and your body will decay. Spiritual exercise, on the other hand, will benefit you not only in this life, but for all eternity." There is nothing worldly or sinful about physical exercise, as long as we place it in proper perspective and do not neglect the other areas of our development.

Jesus also grew intellectually. Again, there is nothing wrong with mental preparation and education in its place; in fact, it is a great blessing.

Jesus grew spiritually. He was our example in prayer and fasting. Jesus had a burden for the lost that took Him to Calvary. He wept over Jerusalem and was moved by the needs of others. Happy Henry would do well to heed the words of the chorus "To Be Like Jesus" and learn to mourn and care for the lost.

Jesus grew in personal relationships. Many times He interacted socially with those around Him. He went to people's homes and ate with them. He was not a social recluse, and yet His interaction with other people never interfered with His spirituality. Almost everywhere He went people followed Him. Jesus loved people. Even though people like Henry can sometimes overemphasize the social area of life, it is still necessary to develop in this area in order to have a balanced life. By his antisocial tendencies, Mournful Mike is being anything but Christlike.

Just like the other issues we have explored in previous chapters, there can be a balance between mourning and joyfulness, introverted spirituality and lukewarm extroversion. As in so many other issues, we can find that balance in Jesus Christ, our great example.

9

Freedom
versus
Authority

"Stand fast therefore in the liberty wherewith Christ hath made us free, and be not entangled again with the yoke of bondage" (Galatians 5:1). On the surface, this verse of Scripture seems to capture the heart's cry of many in the world today who have tasted of the baptism of the Holy Ghost. Take Connie Charismatic for example.

Connie was at one time a member of a mainline denominational church. Bound by tradition and dry ritualism, Connie began to search her Bible as well as countless books written about the Holy Spirit. Some of Connie's friends were introduced to the subject by various "charismatic" television evangelists. Once they received the Holy Ghost, they felt a freedom to worship God as they never had before. This freedom of worship was strongly discouraged by their mainline denominational ministers, who lacked a personal born-again experience. Unwilling to return to the bondage of tradition, these newly Spirit-baptized people severed their former relationships with pastors and churches to revel in their newfound spiritual freedom. They contented themselves by attending lay prayer meetings, listening to cassette tapes, and watching a smorgasbord of television evangelists.

As time went on, many of these new believers made their first contact with an Apostolic Pentecostal church, and such was the case with Connie Charismatic. Invited by a friend, Connie was initially thrilled by what she found. She saw an entire church full of people worshiping and praising God in an uninhibited manner. After months of merely listening to tapes and watching television, she was thrilled beyond measure to see and hear an anointed sermon preached in person. After the message, Connie Charismatic excitedly told the pastor, "I believe I have been led by the Spirit to attend your church."

It is not long, however, until Connie begins to have second thoughts about her decision to commit herself to one church. For one thing, she is beginning to feel guilt and conviction about some habits that still bind her. She never felt conviction like that when she was "free." Connie Charismatic also is having a difficult time grasping the concept of faithfulness, which is taught from the pulpit and mentioned frequently in testimony services. She likes to go to church "as the Spirit leads her." She also wants to pray, read her Bible, and give to God's work "as the Spirit leads her." Unfortunately, the "Spirit" seems to move on her to do these things quite sporadically and inconsistently. Consequently, the very thought of tithing, attending services regularly and consistently, or anything else along those lines makes Connie feel constricted. Above else, Connie values freedom, and she feels that submission to pastoral authority would seriously compromise that freedom.

Before Connie makes her final decision, she does the wisest thing that she could possibly do. She opens her Bible and begins to search the Scriptures. Freedom versus authority—how does God's Word resolve this apparent conflict?

After a few days of intensive study, Connie discovers that the Bible's definition of freedom is not license to do whatever one feels like. There are, in fact, several things that Christian are not "free" to do if they want to please God.

First of all, a Christian is not free to disobey God-given leadership. "Obey them that have the rule over you, and submit yourselves: for they watch for your souls, as they that must give account, that they may do it with joy, and not with grief: for that is unprofitable for you" (Hebrews 13:17). The Bible describes God-called pastors as shepherds who watch over the flock of God. A shepherd leads and sheep follow. "The elders which are among you I exhort, who am also an elder, . . . Feed the flock of God which is among you, taking the oversight thereof, not by constraint, but willingly; not for filthy lucre, but of a ready mind; neither as being lords over God's heritage but being examples to the flock" (I Peter 5:1-3). This role of shepherd carries with it great responsibility and authority. Paul told Timothy to "command and teach" those things he had shared with him (I Timothy 4:11). Jesus, who grants His children freedom, has also ordained spiritual authority in the church.

Second, a Christian is not free to attend church only when he or she feels like it. God warns His children against "forsaking the assembling of ourselves together, as the manner of some is" (Hebrews 10:25). We do not have to fast and pray for a week to find out if it is God's will for us to attend church the next week. The Bible explicitly tells us that if the church assembles together, then we ought to be there.

Third, a Christian is not free to sin; rather, he has been set free *from* sin. He must not continue in the filthy habits of sin after he has been saved. "For, brethren, ye have been called unto liberty; only use not liberty for an occasion to the flesh" (Galatians 5:13). "For the grace of God that bringeth salvation hath appeared to all men, teaching us that, denying ungodliness and worldly lusts, we should live soberly, righteously, and godly, in this present world" (Titus 2:11-12). The conviction Connie feels is a result of the Spirit of God trying to deliver her from the bondage of sin and worldly ways. The preaching of the Word of God creates an atmosphere in which God can move and talk to the hearts of individuals.

It is God's will for us to purify ourselves and leave worldly pollution. "And what agreement hath the temple of God with idols? for ye are the temple of the living God; as God hath said, I will dwell in them, and walk in them; and I will be their God, and they shall be my people. Wherefore come out from among them, and be ye separate, saith the Lord, and touch not the unclean thing; and I will receive you" (II Corinthians 6:16-17). The freedom that Christ gives most definitely is not a freedom to sin.

Finally, a Christian is not free to live in such a manner that could cause a brother or sister in the Lord to stumble and fall. Every Christian has a responsibility to those around him. "We then that are strong ought to bear the infirmities of the weak, and not to please ourselves" (Romans 15:1).

True spiritual freedom is not the right to do anything someone feels like doing whenever he wants to. Connie now readily sees that fact. Then what is freedom? Freedom is the power to do what we know is right, to do what is best for us spiritually. Jesus said, "Ye shall know the truth, and the truth shall make you free" (John 8:32). He came to free us from the awful oppression of sin that kept us from doing what was right, for "whosoever committeth sin is the servant of sin" (John 8:34). In other words, Christ sets us free to enable us to submit to a higher authority and thereby inherit eternal life.

Before salvation, we submitted to the whims of the flesh, but now we are capable of following the Spirit. "There is therefore now no condemnation to them which are in Christ Jesus, who walk not after the flesh, but after the Spirit. For the law of the Spirit of life in Christ Jesus hath made me free from the law of sin and death" (Romans 8:1-2).

Somewhere in the soul of Connie Charismatic (or perhaps we should say Connie Christian) a light is turned on. There is now no conflict between freedom and spiritual authority. By liberating us from the tyranny of fleshly, carnal desires, Jesus Christ enables us to follow spiritual authority: the Holy Spirit, the Word of God, and God-called pastors and teachers who proclaim and apply the principles of God's Word.

Connie decides that with the help of God she is going

to be faithful to the precepts of His Word. It will not always be easy for the flesh, but Jesus promised, "If the Son therefore shall make you free, ye shall be free indeed" (John 8:36).

10

Gospel Music: Frenzy
versus
Boredom

Due to cultural differences and personal tastes, music has always varied in style and quality from region to region and church to church. Some churches like the twangy sounds of gospel bluegrass. Others dislike the Southern gospel sound and prefer slower, "deeper" songs. As one man from Arkansas explained to me, "Yankees talk fast and sing slow; Southerners talk slow and sing fast." Some enjoy black gospel, and some prefer a middle-of-the-road sound. In recent times, however, a new influence has pervaded gospel music, namely, rock music. Some musicians, youth leaders, and even pastors have seemingly taken the stance of "If you can't beat them, join them" toward rock music. The lyrics are changed, of course, but the heavy beat and overall musical style stay the same.

It is most disturbing for those who were avid rock

listeners before their conversion to be exposed to so-called Christian rock. The music often reminds them of their past involvement with the things rock music is closely associated with: drugs, alcohol, the occult, wild parties, and immoral lifestyles. Pity the poor individual who travels to a camp meeting or youth rally expecting to be spiritually uplifted when a hotshot group struts to the platform with heavily amplified instruments and begins to lay down a heavy beat that would make the Rolling Stones turn green with envy.

In such a case, the lyrics of the song are barely heard above the heavy bass and drumbeat. The singers and musicians may move and jerk in a way that shows they are more in tune with the rock music beat than with the Spirit of God. They may act as performers seeking adulation rather than as worshipers and worship leaders. Some have gone so far as to take a rock hit and change a few of the lyrics to "convert" it to gospel. Thus "C'mon, baby, let's rock the town tonight" becomes "C'mon, children, let's praise the Lord tonight." As muffled as the lyrics are, however, most of these groups could sing the original song without anyone being the wiser.

The most tragic aspect of using hard rock in the church is that it fails to accomplish the very purpose of music: it does not inspire worship of Jesus Christ. But everyone who speaks or ministers (or sings in church) should do so "that God in all things may be glorified through Jesus Christ, to whom be praise and dominion for ever and ever. Amen" (I Peter 4:11). Almost without exception, after a group performs a rock song at a camp or rally, there is very little, if any, worship inspired. Instead, the congregation usually applauds the performance and performers. The custom of applauding the group is relatively new in Pentecostal circles, but it is rapidly becoming prevalent in some areas. Perhaps it seems harmless, but according to Romans 1:25-26, one of the first steps in turning away from God is to worship and serve the creature instead of the Creator.

Throughout the Book of Psalms we see that God's intention for music was to glorify Him: "Praise him with the sound of the trumpet: praise him with the psaltery and harp" (Psalm 150:3). The playing of instruments and singing are meant to praise God, to bring glory to Him. Rock music tends to exalt the performer, not the Savior. The strong, rhythmic beat and heavy bass tones of hard rock music excite the carnal nature of easily stimulated youth. Tacking Christian lyrics to rock does not change the effect of the music. Popular modern rock groups drive crowds of young people into a frenzy with the driving beat of their music. No one can hear the lyrics over the screams of the fans, but it matters little, for there is a message in the beat itself.

Dare we try to incorporate the hard rock sound into our music? Contrary to the instructions in the law of Moses, King David and the Israelites tried to use ox carts to carry the ark of the covenant back to Jerusalem. The use of this Philistine method of transporting the ark proved to be disastrous; it resulted in the death of Uzzah. Some have thought that using a heavy rock style in gospel music helps communicate the gospel message to young people. But dare we carry this holy message on Philistine ox carts?

On the other hand, the use of rock music in churches has spawned an unfortunate countertrend. Many churches, offended and disgusted by the heavy rock beat used by some gospel groups, have retreated to the opposite extreme of the musical spectrum. To escape frenzy they embrace boredom.

These churches become so overly concerned about too much rhythm and beat that their music takes on traditional denominational overtones. Their choirs sing dull, uninspired, out-of-date material that would be more appropriate for a mainline denominational choir. To avoid the spectre of rock, they rob their music of any liveliness and excitement at all. Pentecostals, after all, have always been known for their lively, spirited music. People were clapping their hands and tapping their toes in Pentecostal churches long before Elvis Presley, Bill Haley, and others introduced rock-and-roll to the world.

In fact, it is ironic that rock in its beginning stole heavily from gospel music. Elvis Presley, whose musical background included gospel singing and trinitarian Pentecostal camp meetings, took the basic excitement of gospel and incorporated it into his singing style. Other popular performers, particularly some of the black artists, began as gospel singers.

Clearly, then, we can and should avoid the heavy beat and overaccentuated rhythm of rock without stripping gospel music of any trace of beat and rhythm at all. A gospel group should not sound like the Rolling Stones, but then again, it does not have to sound like performers in a cathedral. Frenzy versus boredom—are these the only alternatives for gospel music? The answer is a resounding no, provided certain principles are upheld in the use of music.

First and foremost, music must serve the purpose of

leading people into the worship of God. As a choir, group, or individual plays or sings unto the Lord, the feeling projected should be "Isn't the Lord good? Let us worship Jesus. Thank You, Jesus." It should not be "Aren't I talented? Don't I have a beautiful voice? Aren't you impressed by my musical skill?" Jesus must be at the center of our worship. The question must be asked: Does this song lift up Jesus—does it lead people to worship Him? If not, it is not appropriate for congregational worship. This question is more important than how professional and polished the music is.

At the same time, there is no rule that says the sloppier the presentation, the more spiritual it is. "Sing unto him a new song; play skilfully with a loud noise" (Psalm 33:3). Singers and musicians should sing and play as skilfully as possible. They must beware, however, lest they become so concerned about polish that they neglect prayer. Music in church must have a spiritual impact or it is useless. We do not come to church to be entertained; we come to be spiritually uplifted. First and foremost, music must inspire worship.

Second, the lyrics of our music must not be garbled or overpowered by the music. Music need not be slow—it can at times be lively—but the lyrics should be clearly understood by everyone. The strength of a good gospel song is not tricky beats or outrageous rhythms, but strong, uplifting lyrics.

The third principle depends on the singers and the musicians themselves. It is important for them not to allow Satan to puff up their ego because of their talent. Many rock performers are some of the most egotistical individuals who have ever lived. If Christian musicians allow themselves to listen to the perverted rock music of today, they may soon find themselves emulating the egotistical performances of those rock performers in their music. They must not let rock taint their talent. If they do not listen to it, they will not be tempted to imitate it. The path to spiritual success is to stay humble, pray to God, and ask Him to move on people's hearts through the music. After all, what good is a note-perfect song performed in church if it does not have the blessings of God on it? Let us ask God to bless our talents and use them for His glory.

The Pentecostal experience is unique, and Pentecostal music should be unique also. We do not need or want the taint of rock in our music. We have the Holy Ghost to move people; we do not need a carnal beat to do so. On the other hand, we are not straight-jacketed by formalism either. Our music throbs with the life of the Spirit of God. We can sing "He Touched Me" in slow heartfelt worship to God, and then sing "I've Got It" with great emotion and enthusiasm, worshiping God just as sincerely with both.

Frenzy versus boredom? The choice does not have to be either/or; it can be neither/nor. May we never be forced to embrace either extreme, but may our music remain the unique music of a unique people called out of formalism and sensual carnality to declare praises unto Jesus Christ. "Ye are a chosen generation, a royal priesthood, an holy nation, a peculiar people; that ye should shew forth the praises of him who hath called you out of darkness into his marvelous light" (I Peter 2:9).

11

End-time Apostasy
versus
End-time Revival

M ost Pentecostals agree wholeheartedly that we are living in the last days. They have seen Israel restored as a nation and other prophecies come to pass during the last forty years. There is a strong feeling in our fellowship that the Second Coming of Jesus Christ is very near.

There are, however, some differences of opinion over what to expect between now and the rapture of the church. Will the church experience a great, sweeping revival or will it fall into apostasy with only a faithful few left ready for the Rapture?

Let us first examine the position of those who expect end-time apostasy. Jesus spoke to His disciples concerning the last days in Matthew 24. In verse 12 He prophesied, "And because iniquity shall abound, the love of many shall wax cold." A similar and even more explicit picture of the latter days is revealed in II Timothy 3:1-5: "This know also, that in the last days perilous times shall come. For men shall be lovers of their own selves, covetous, boasters, proud, blasphemers, disobedient to parents, unthankful, unholy, without natural affection, trucebreakers, false accusers, incontinent, fierce, despisers of those that are good, traitors, heady, highminded, lovers of pleasures more than lovers of God; having a form of godliness, but denying the power thereof: from such turn away."

The description of the Laodicean church found in Revelation 3 provides a picture of apostasy. Laodicea was the last of the seven churches of Asia Minor to be mentioned, and some have thereby concluded that it is particularly representative of the last portion of the church age. "I know thy works, that thou art neither cold nor hot: I would thou were cold or hot. So then because thou art lukewarm, and neither cold nor hot, I will spue thee out of my mouth. Because thou sayest, I am rich, and increased with goods, and have need of nothing; and knowest not that thou art wretched, and miserable, and poor, and blind, and naked" (Revelation 3:15-17).

Given the weight of these and other passages of Scripture such as II Peter 3:3-4 and Jude 11:21, some people expect a great end-time apostasy and take a dim view of the possibility of a sweeping revival before the Rapture. Yet what about the churches that are experiencing revival? Is there a scriptural basis for end-time revival?

There is the promise of a latter rain. "Be patient therefore, brethren, unto the coming of the Lord. Behold, the husbandman waiteth for the precious fruit of the earth, and hath long patience for it until he receive the early and latter rain" (James 5:7). Other passages that mention the early and latter rain are Hosea 6:3, Joel 2:23, and Zechariah 10:1.

The early, or former, rain falls in Israel in autumn, right after the planting of seed. Because it was the first period of rainfall in the agricultural cycle, it very important. It is superceded in importance, however, by what is called the latter rain. The latter rain is considered greater than the former rain for two reasons. First of all, the latter rainfall is usually much heavier than the former. Second, the latter rain falls just prior to the harvest.

The observation in James 3 is quite significant when considered in the light of church history. The first outpouring of the Holy Ghost, or the former rain, took place on the Day of Pentecost and throughout the Book of Acts. This rainfall soon tapered off to a time of slight drizzle throughout the Middle Ages. Now, however, with the time of harvest (Rapture) drawing near, the rainfall has resumed in earnest. If the latter rain is greater and heavier than the former rain, and if the Rapture of the church, a time of spiritual harvest, is really as near as most think it is, it is logical to assume that it will be immediately preceded by a latter-rain outpouring of the Holy Ghost.

Jesus, who certainly knew what conditions would prevail in the last days, gave the command, "Go ye therefore, and teach all nations," and with this command He also gave a promise: "Lo, I am with you alway, even unto the end of the world" (Matthew 28:19-20). The phrase "end of the world" has reference to time, not geography, and could be better translated as "end of the age."

That Jesus expected the church to experience revival

up to the very end is shown by the prophecy He gave in Matthew 24:14: "And this gospel of the kingdom shall be preached in all the world for a witness unto all nations; and then shall the end come." Obviously there will be saints living in the end times whose love will not wax cold and who will still be sharing the gospel with the lost.

The church was built upon a rock, and Jesus declared that "the gates of hell shall not prevail against it" (Matthew 16:18). For the entire church to apostasize in the last days would mean that the gates of hell had prevailed. But I Thessalonians 4:17 assures us that there will be saints who are "alive and remain" at the coming of the Lord. And the apostle Peter declared on the Day of Pentecost, "For the promise is unto you, and to your children, and to all that are afar off, even as many as the Lord our God shall call" (Acts 2:39).

I, for one, am glad that over nineteen hundred years after Peter preached that promise and in the middle of a world in which theologians had begun to declare that God was dead, the living God called me and filled me with the Holy Ghost. Though I certainly was "afar off" in terms of time and space, God was still pouring out His Spirit.

Thus, the question must be asked, How do we reconcile the passages of Scripture that point to apostasy and lukewarmness in the end times with the scriptural concept of latter-rain, end-time revival? What is the proper, balanced perspective? To better understand the church in its last stage, let us examine the church in its beginning.

The early apostolic church had people of the caliber of Peter, James, John, and Barnabas; yet it also had Ananias and Sapphira. The Apostle Paul traveled the globe in his zeal for Christ, but Demos forsook Paul and the church because of a love for the world. Jude wrote an epistle warning the church of ungodly men who had crept in the church unawares and were turning the grace of God into a license for sin and denying the only Lord God. All of this happened in the early church.

Will it be any different in the last days? Is it not possible that while some will fall prey to Laodicean lukewarmness others will "ask . . . of the LORD rain in the time of the latter rain" (Zechariah 10:1)?

It is wise to be cautious and to be aware of what Satan is trying to do to the church in these the last days of time. Paul wrote the Thessalonians concerning the end times, "But ye, brethren, are not in darkness, that that day should overtake you as a thief. Ye are all the children of light, and the children of the day: we are not of the night, nor of darkness. Therefore let us not sleep, as do others; but let us watch and be sober" (I Thessalonians 5:4-6). It is wise to note evil trends and be watchful, but not to the point of letting caution steal our faith in God. It is possible that, while guarding against evil, we could lose the proper perspective.

Elijah is an example of someone who lost his perspective in the face of evil. In I Kings 19 the great prophet Elijah, who had just experienced a stunning victory over 450 prophets of Baal, sat down under a juniper tree and asked God to let him die. Later in that chapter we can almost hear the whine in his voice as he complained to God, "I have been very jealous for the LORD God of hosts: because the children of Israel have forsaken thy covenant, thrown down thine altars, and slain thy prophets with the sword; and I, even I only, am left; and they seek my life, to take it away" (I Kings 19:14).

We can summarize or loosely paraphrase God's

answer to Elijah as follows: What's the matter with you, Elijah? Get out of this cave and get on your way to the wilderness of Damascus; I've got some work for you to do. You're so concerned about what Baal's boys are doing that you've forgotten that *My* program's in full swing. Besides, I have seven thousand people in Israel who haven't worshiped Baal; so quit feeling like the Lone Ranger and do My will." (See I Kings 19:15-18.)

Sadly enough, in these troubled times, there seem to be some people who, like Elijah, start feeling like the Lone Ranger. They mope under their juniper trees, too depressed by what Satan is doing to do anything for God. Teach a home Bible study? Pray and fast for revival? Witness to a lost soul? You can almost hear them moan, "What's the use? This world is so wicked—nobody wants to live for God. Churches are compromising, people are backsliding—why, everyone knows God's not blessing like He did in the good old days. It's bad and it's gonna get worse. I'm just gonna sit tight and wait for the Rapture."

To these modern-day Elijahs, I believe the Spirit of the Lord is exhorting: "Get up and get going. Yes, these are wicked times, and yes, there are those who are growing cold. I am still in control, however, and there are many saints who are still standing strong and have not compromised. Meanwhile, there are millions of lost people who are hungering for the message I have placed into your hands. Go, witness, pray, fast, and preach, and I will send revival in your midst. Those who hunger and thirst after righteousness shall be filled. Ask for rain in the time of latter rain."

Apostasy versus revival? One or the other? No, *both* will happen as prophesied in the Scripture. Whether we experience revival or fall prey to apostasy is up to us.

12

Personality
versus
Principle

It is a quiet and peaceful Saturday night in the slumbering little town of Thomasville. Parked in front of the Thomas Men's Store, right across from the Thomas Pharmacy, is the sheriff. He has stretched out in his patrol car and is just about to nod off with boredom, when suddenly, like an explosion, a Cadillac DeVille roars down Main Street at about a hundred miles per hour. The huge vehicle weaves erratically from left to right, and only the fact that the street is deserted saves the streaking vehicle from certain destruction.

Now the quiet of the little town is shattered by the wail of a siren as a very upset sheriff, clutching the wheel of his patrol car angrily, catches up with the offending vehicle and pulls it over. "You reckless idiot," the sheriff mutters as he approaches the offending vehicle. "You might as well plan on spending the night in jail." The sheriff's flashlight beam catches the bloodshot eyes of the obviously inebriated, red-faced man who stumbles angrily out of his car. "You got a problem or something, Offisher?" The man smiles at the stunned reaction of the young sheriff.

"No sir, Mr. Thomas. How are you tonight, sir? I didn't recognize the new car, sir. I'm sorry I bothered you." Very hurriedly he places the ticket he had planned to write in his pocket. "Good night, sir. Have a safe trip home."

"Oh, boy, by the way, did you clock me with your radar?" Mr. Thomas, owner of about three-fourths of Thomasville, asks with a grin.

"Yes sir, you were doing one hundred in a twenty-miles-per-hour zone."

"Thanks, son," and with that Mr. Thomas resumes his reckless journey homeward.

Personality versus principle. How many times, in how many ways, has principle come up a bloody and bowed loser to personality, just as it did that night in our fictional town of Thomasville? Fortunately, principle always wins over personality with us born-again believers—right?

Perhaps the question should be asked, Are principles more important than personality? In other words, if something is wrong, it is wrong no matter who does it? Is truth truth and error error, no matter how attractive or unattractive the people are on either side?

Actually, the Bible is very explicit in its condemnation of favoritism or respect of persons. The Bible is a book of principles that do not bend in favor of persons. "You shall do no injustice in judgment. You shall not be partial to the poor, nor honor the person of the mighty.

But in righteousness you shall judge your neighbor" (Leviticus 19:15, NKJV). "You shall not show partiality in judgment; you shall hear the small as well as the great; you shall not be afraid in any man's presence, for the judgment is God's" (Deuteronomy 1:17, NKJV). "I charge thee before God, and the Lord Jesus Christ, and the elect angels, that thou observe these things without preferring one before another, doing nothing by partiality" (I Timothy 5:21).

It is obvious from these and other verses of Scripture that God warns against the all-too-human tendency to show partiality and to place personality above principle. That Paul had to charge Timothy along these lines demonstrates that having the Holy Ghost does not make us immune from this problem and that even ministers are not invulnerable to the lure of partiality.

Dr. James Dobson, noted child psychologist and author, referred in his book *Hide and Seek* to the characteristics that people most highly esteem. He called beauty the gold coin and intelligence the silver coin of human value. In other words, we are often swayed by beauty and intelligence. Who hasn't known, a witty charmer who seems to know how to talk his way out of trouble, or a pert little beauty who knows how to bat her long lashes and shed a few crocodile tears from her baby blue eyes, thus melting the hearts of those who would correct her?

In the realm of the church, perhaps we should consider three other coins of human value that have potential to sway us from unbiased judgment. These three are wealth, talent, and success.

Let us first consider wealth. James warned against

playing favorites because of financial status: "For if there should come into your assembly a man with gold rings, in fine apparel, and there should also come in a poor man with filthy clothes, and you pay attention to the one wearing the fine clothes and say to him, 'You sit here in a good place,' and say to the poor man, 'You stand there,' or, 'Sit here at my footstool,' have you not shown partiality among yourselves, and become judges with evil thoughts? . . . If you show partiality, you commit sin" (James 2:2-4, 9, NKJV).

The church is holy, and it must never have two sets of standards—one for the wealthy and another for the poor. Moreover, an individual's wealth or lack of wealth should not affect our witnessing to him. Every one needs Jesus Christ and salvation regardless of his or her financial status. A Pentecostal church should be a place where the richest and the poorest people in town can come and be loved by the people and directed to Jesus Christ. May our churches be free of all snob appeal *and* slob appeal. In God's sight neither the rich nor the poor are honored above others.

It should also be pointed out that the spirituality and success of a church cannot be judged according to the church's financial assets. There are spiritually bankrupt churches that own acres of land and gorgeous facilities, and there are vibrant, spiritually dynamic churches that must meet in less than ideal circumstances. Of course, dilapidated buildings do not guarantee a spiritual congregation any more than beautiful facilities indicate lukewarm, compromising congregations. Wealth rains on the just and the unjust. Wealth itself neither justifies nor condemns anyone in the sight of God.

Let us now look at the second coin called talent. Our expressive worship of God, with its natural emphasis on musical and vocal expression to God, opens up many opportunities for the talented in our midst to shine. This situation is not necessarily bad in itself, for everyone should strive to utilize his talents for the kingdom of God. However, we must be careful not to exaggerate the worth of an individual by basing it on talent. There are very precious and wonderful saints of God who are invaluable to the church even though they cannot play a musical instrument, sing like a bird, act in a drama, or give a spellbinding testimony. There are—believe it or not— minister's wives who are tremendous blessings to their churches and husbands yet who cannot play a piano, organ, or accordion. Like wealth, talent neither commends nor condemns a person before God. It is rather how faithfully and honorably someone uses his talents that commends him to God.

Sadly, some feel that an abundance of talent gives them certain privileges. Satan has a way of puffing up our egos if we let him. Thus, some think, "How dare the pastor talk to *me* that way. I know the pastor across town would give his right arm to have a piano player like me in his church." Every instruction and ordinance of God applies to everyone, regardless of what talent he possesses. Whatever it takes for Tone Deaf Tommy to make the Rapture, it will also take for Michael Maestro to go.

"I know that what he's preaching isn't in the Bible. I know he's promoted a lot of false doctrine, but . . . look how big his church is. Look how many visitors he has every Sunday in his multimillion-dollar cathedral. If he's wrong why is he so successful?" The tremendous persuasive power of "success" is very obvious every time we hear such a confused cry.

Unfortunately, we often judge success by a different standard than God does. We look at the outward appearance, but God looks at the heart. On the surface, the church of Laodicea appeared to be a smashing success. The people were rich, had many possessions, and had need of nothing. God looked past all that, however, and saw that spiritually they were wretched, miserable, poor, blind, and naked.

The size or earthly success of individuals or churches neither commends them nor condemns them. Some churches grow because they sincerely desire to grow and are doing things that are pleasing in the sight of God. Others grow numerically by compromise and skillful personal relations. Both seem to achieve the same end, but they have different destinies. The same is true of individuals. The truly successful person or church is the one that is successful on God's terms. The house built by the wise man (on obedience to the Word of God) will stand in the time of the storm; the house of the foolish man will surely fall.

No discussion of the conflict between principle and personality would be complete without contemplating Paul's rebuke of Peter. (See Galatians 2:11-14.) Paul rebuked Peter face to face because Peter would have fellowship with the Gentiles as long as his friends weren't around, but when some of his Jewish friends showed up he began to snub the Gentile believers. This attitude of Peter's affected others, and they to began to snub the Gentiles. To Paul, wrong was wrong, no matter who was involved. On a *principle,* he openly corrected Peter.

There are times when principle must be separated from personality. Many have been known to dodge a principle by complaining, "This disagreement is a personal vendetta—people just don't like me and they're out to get me." May we never become afraid to uphold godly principles for fear of bruising a sensitive personality. Paul had no ill feeling toward Peter personally, but he wasn't about to watch wrongdoing and keep quiet about it; Paul took a stand on the matter.

It is to Peter's credit that he never attempted to pull rank on Paul to justify himself. Peter could have said, "Well, I've been in this way a lot longer than you, and when you were out throwing believers in jail, I was preaching the truth." But Peter accepted the admonition, not as a personal attack, but as a loving correction based on sound Christian principle. He allowed principle to overrule personality.

Principle versus personality—when this conflict arises, the church must always choose principle.

Part Two

Anatomy
of a
Backslider

1

A Spiritual Autopsy

The preacher walked briskly to his car from the graveside. He paused and then turned to take one last, forlorn look behind him. His wife, sensing his frustration and sadness, tenderly touched his arm and said, "Honey, you preached the best funeral message that you could, especially when you consider the circumstances."

The preacher stared vacantly at the casket that was poised to fill its final resting place. It's not easy, he thought to himself, to preach the funeral of a backslider. Oh, how he hated even the sound of that word, *backslider!* In all the years he had been a pastor, he could not grasp what made people turn their back on God and embrace the world again. Tom, where did you go wrong? his heart cried.

He blinked as his eyes rebelled against the sudden burst of light that surrounded him. Stunned, he found himself sitting in a lecture hall with walls of pure white. Gone was the car, the cemetery, and his wife. He looked up and saw a tall figure of noble bearing standing before a lectern in front of the hall.

Before he could ask a question concerning his whereabouts, the figure began to speak. "Welcome, Pastor. The results of our spiritual autopsy are complete. We have transported you here temporarily in order to instruct you concerning the anatomy of a backslider. Perhaps you can help others not to repeat the mistakes that proved spiritually fatal to Tom. Please direct your attention to the screen to my left. In a few moments we will examine the anatomy of a backslider. Before we do, let us first examine what the term *backsliding* really means."

• • • • •

When a person is born into the kingdom of God he renounces his own selfish, carnal impulses and begins to be led by the Spirit of God. "For as many as are led by the Spirit of God, they are the sons of God" (Romans 8:14).

Let us picture a large cow being led by a farmer. As long as that cow willingly follows the farmer, the farmer has no problem leading the cow. If the cow balks, however, the farmer can no longer effectively lead. God used Hosea to show Israel how she had acted "as a backsliding heifer" (Hosea 4:16). Like an obstinate cow, Israel refused to be led by God. Instead, Israel chose to turn away from God's love and instruction.

Backsliding can be defined as a negative response or series of responses to the leading of the Spirit. It usually results in the rebellious individual's return to the pollutions of the world. The apostle Peter described the awful consequences awaiting a person who draws back from the Christian life: "For if after they have escaped the pollutions of the world through the knowledge of the Lord and

88

Saviour Jesus Christ, they are again entangled therein, and overcome, the latter end is worse with them than the beginning. For it had been better for them not to have known the way of righteousness, than, after they have known it, to turn from the holy commandment delivered unto them. But it is happened unto them according to the true proverb, The dog is turned to his own vomit again; and the sow that was washed to her wallowing in the mire" (II Peter 2:20-22).

It is possible for a backslider to reconsider his position and return to God. The parable of the prodigal son is a prime example. Yet it cannot be emphasized enough that there is no guarantee that the backslider will in fact return.

The Book of Ruth tells the story of a family that left Bethlehem during a time of famine to dwell in Moab. Of the four who departed, only Naomi lived to return home to Bethlehem; her husband and two sons died and were buried in Moab. Although God in His mercy gave Naomi a precious daughter-in-law, Ruth, she still had to contend with life-long memories of tombstones in Moab.

Who knows how many tombstones are in Moab today? How many people have left the church intending one day to return to God, only to die in a backslidden condition? The tragedy of these "tombstones in Moab" is that backsliding is so foolish and unnecessary. No external force or circumstance—natural or supernatural—can ever separate someone from the love and grace of God. A person backslides because he *chooses* to backslide. Thus backsliding can also be defined as a decision or series of decisions to turn from God back toward sin.

Now that we understand the term *backsliding* better, we will next examine the anatomy of a backslider.

2

A Head Empty
of Knowledge

" "P astor, several factors evidently contributed to
the spiritual demise of your former saint, Tom.
We will go over each one of these factors with you in the
hope that you will be able to help others not to repeat
Tom's fatal mistakes."

The anatomy of a backslider almost always includes
an empty head. The Lord spoke to a backslidden Israel
in Hosea 4:6: "My people are destroyed for lack of
knowledge: because thou hast rejected knowledge, I will
also reject thee, that thou shalt be no priest to me."

As wonderful as the initial experience with God is,
it is vital that a convert go on to learn of the ways of God.
Peter admonished Christians to add to their faith virtue,
and to virtue knowledge (II Peter 1:5).

It only takes one book of the New Testament, the
Book of Acts, to present the New Testament salvation
experience. In only a few minutes anyone can learn of
his need to repent, be baptized in Jesus' name, and receive

the gift of the Holy Spirit. Yet to teach us how to walk with Him in the Christian life, God allotted twenty-one books of the New Testament, the Epistles. Learning how to be effective disciples of Christ is a lifetime proposition of seeking out knowledge of God's ways, which are not like the ways of humanity.

The true test of a disciple is whether or not he is willing to continue on in the Word of God. There is more to the Bible than John 3:16 and Acts 2:38. Jesus states in John 8:31, "If ye continue in my word, then are ye my disciples indeed; and ye shall know the truth, and the truth shall make you free."

A surprising number of people who sit in the pews of Pentecostal churches know little or next to nothing about the Bible beyond Acts 2:38. Between services, their Bibles lie unopened in the back seat of their cars or on their dressers. The only time they read their Bibles is when the preacher reads his text for the sermon. Apparently they do not believe what God declared through the prophet Isaiah: "Therefore my people are gone into captivity, because they have no knowledge" (Isaiah 5:13).

For a time, a new Christian can seemingly get along fine without any real knowledge of God's Word. He can attend church, worship, rejoice, and ride a wave of emotions. But if worship in spirit is not balanced by worship in truth—which requires a knowledge of God's Word—it will produce a shallow and carnal Christian.

Worship is important, and our experience with God will produce powerful emotions. It is the Word of God, however, that has the power to cut out the deep, deceitful sins of the heart. "For the word of God is quick, and powerful, and sharper than any twoedged sword, piercing even to the dividing asunder of soul and spirit . . . and is a discerner of the thoughts and intents of the heart" (Hebrews 4:12). "Wherewithal shall a young man cleanse his way? by taking heed thereto according to thy word. With my whole heart have I sought thee: O let me not wander from thy commandments. Thy word have I hid in mine heart, that I might not sin against thee" (Psalm 119:9-11).

A love for truth and a thirst for spiritual knowledge are sure vaccines against the possibility of backsliding. A person who has walked with God for a number of years and has remained steadfast is invariably someone who has become knowledgeable of God's Word. On the other hand, a person who has fallen away from the grace of God is usually someone who never bothered to study the deeper things of God.

If only Tom would have heeded the Apostle Paul's advice to Timothy: "Study to shew thyself approved unto God, a workman that needeth not to be ashamed, rightly dividing the word of truth" (II Timothy 2:15). Knowledge of God's Word would certainly have helped Tom not to stray away from God. Unfortunately, ignorance, not knowledge, is a characteristic associated with the backslider. Even though God desired Tom to be saved and to come to the knowledge of the truth—as He does everyone (I Timothy 2:4)—Tom chose instead to walk in darkness and ignorance. It cost him his soul.

The backslider has more than just an empty head. He also has an upturned nose—a sure indication of a life full of pride. Next we will examine the role that pride plays in the anatomy of a backslider.

3

A Nose Turned Up
by Pride

"Pastor, our spiritual autopsy showed that Tom was severely afflicted by an upturned nose. Pride is almost always part of the spiritual anatomy of a backslider, and Tom proved to be no exception."

The preacher began to remember Tom's early days in the church. How humble he had been in the beginning! So many people realize when they are first saved how fortunate they are to know Jesus Christ. They appreciate how wonderful God's plan of salvation is. The prevailing attitude is "I am so thankful Jesus called me out of sin into His marvelous light."

When people are humble they are also teachable and easily entreated. In the early days of Tom's walk with God, his pastor had only to hint that correction was in order and Tom was quick to comply. A humble person feels it is his privilege to attend church, give to God's cause, and work for God. After all, without God's mercy he would be lost. He feels indebted to the Lord and His church.

This attitude of humility and indebtedness must be carefully maintained throughout a person's walk with God; otherwise, a subtle change of attitude can occur. Instead of a person feeling indebted to God, the church, and the ministry, he can begin to believe that God, the church, and the ministry should feel indebted to him. He can begin to feel proud about his spiritual accomplishments.

Jesus gave an apt illustration of spiritual pride in Luke 18:11-12: "The Pharisee stood and prayed thus with himself, God, I thank thee, that I am not as other men are, extortioners, unjust, adulterers, or even as this publican. I fast twice in the week, I give tithes of all I possess."

It was not the tax collectors and sinners who persecuted Jesus; it was the supposedly religious but certainly proud Pharisees who caused the most heartache for the Master. It is not usually the sinner who tears a pastor's heart out and tramples on his dignity. It is instead a "saint of God," intoxicated with pride and self-righteousness, who takes it upon himself to rebuke and resist God's anointed one.

Is there trouble in the local church? Is there someone who continually challenges the motives and intent of the pastor? If so, the people need to heed the words of Solomon: "He that is of a proud heart stirreth up strife" (Proverbs 28:25).

Pride will cause people to feel that they are indispensable to the kingdom of God. They begin to feel that without their money and their labors the church would surely fold.

Pride also blinds people to their own spiritual lack: "Thou sayest, I am rich, and increased with goods, and have need of nothing; and knowest not that thou art wretched, and miserable, and poor, and blind, and naked" (Revelation 3:17).

A certain young man attended Bible college shortly after he was converted. He quit after his first year because "they can't teach me anything I don't already know." After returning home he soon "discovered" that, lo and behold, his pastor couldn't really teach him anything either. He moved out of state to attend the church of a "super pastor" who had given him an unethical invitation. He became "superspiritual." He spoke disdainfully of his old church and pastor and their backward ways. One year later this young man's marriage was shattered, and he was back in sin.

The prophet Hosea declared to a backslidden Israel, "And the pride of Israel doth testify to his face: therefore shall Israel and Ephraim fall in their iniquity; Judah also shall fall with them" (Hosea 5:5). Pride has a way of distorting a person's perspective. The Israelites swaggered with pride because they were the chosen children of Abraham, even while they embraced the abominable idols and practices of the heathen whom they felt superior to. They took the blessings of God for granted and offered polluted sacrifices upon the altar.

One lady used to take it upon herself to confront all new converts and haughtily admonish them, "Bless God, we believe in holiness around here, and you'd better straighten up." Finally, the pastor asked her in a kind but firm manner to allow him to instruct the new converts in the ways of holiness. She screamed, stomped out of the church, and by the next weekend was hopping from bar to bar.

The Scriptures declare, "Pride goeth before destruction, and an haughty spirit before a fall" (Proverbs 16:18). A person who forgets where God brought him from is on shaky spiritual ground indeed. The know-it-all, the one who feels he has all the answers, is in danger. "When pride cometh, then cometh shame: but with the lowly is wisdom" (Proverbs 11:2).

Those who have consistently walked with God a long time are people who have maintained a humble attitude. The sermons still speak to them. They still feel there is much to learn. They are not apt to brag about how long they have been in the way, unless it is to boast of God's wonderful keeping power. Above all, they heed the admonition of Romans 12:16: "Be not wise in your own conceits."

If only Tom had continued in the humble manner of his first few months of spiritual walk. Instead, he gradually changed from being grateful to arrogant, from being thankful to grudging. His pastor had noticed these changes and had repeatedly tried to warn Tom, but pride caused these warnings to fall on deaf ears.

Pride was certainly not the only thing that contributed to the spiritual demise of Tom, yet it was a major factor. In addition to pride, a close examination of the mouth revealed that instability and hypocrisy were also present, which we will examine next.

4

A Mouth Examination
Reveals Instability

" " P astor, it is time to continue our analysis of the anatomy of a backslider. In our previous lectures we examined the contributing factors of pride and a lack of knowledge in the spiritual demise of your former saint, Tom. In addition, an examination of Tom's mouth revealed a disparity between words and conduct, and thus hypocrisy and instability. Today, then, we will discuss how instability contributes to the spiritual deterioration of a person caught in the throes of backsliding."

Jesus described spiritual instability in His parable of the sower: "But he who received the seed on stony places, this is he who hears the word and immediately receives it with joy; yet he has no root in himself, but endures only for a while. For when tribulation or persecution arises because of the word, immediately he stumbles" (Matthew 13:20-21, NKJV).

The kind of person Jesus described seems to accept the gospel enthusiastically. All outward appearances indicate that this person has made a solid commitment to Christ, yet somehow those commitments fade in the face of adversity or criticism. Such people tend to conform to the attitudes of the people around them. Placed with spiritual people, they try to act spiritual; but place them with carnal people, and they fall into carnality. This pattern of spiritual instability will inevitably begin to erode their walk with God.

Instability in a person's spiritual life is not always easy to detect at first. People who backslide usually leave in their wake several astonished individuals who shake their heads in disbelief at the news of what seems to them to be the sudden departure of their backslidden brother or sister. They are astonished because they heard Brother Backslider stir the church with dynamic testimonies. They saw him worship loudly and pray fervently. They remember how he spoke so convincingly of his burden for lost souls.

On the other hand, almost without exception there will be others who show little or no surprise about Brother Backslider's fall. They have observed the life of the departed over a period of time and noticed some inconsistencies. Yes, they heard Brother Backslider's dynamic testimonies too. Unfortunately they also heard his critical remarks and his off-color attempts at humor. They saw the demonstrative worship and prayer, but sadly, they also couldn't help but notice the many services he missed for the flimsiest of reasons.

Many a pastor over the years has learned the truth contained in Proverbs 20:6: "Most men will proclaim each his own goodness, but who can find a faithful man?" (NKJV). This proverb captures the essence of a person who allows instability in his life. It is much easier to talk about prayer than it is to actually pray. It is one thing to talk about winning souls and it is another thing altogether to spend the time and effort needed to actually win a soul.

It is amazing how some people can loudly proclaim their love for their church and their pastor and almost in their next breath blast both with withering criticism. Unstable people not only amaze but exasperate and frustrate those who truly practice what they preach.

Evidently, even God can become exasperated with the instability of some of His people. In Hosea 6:4, God confronted His people with their instability: "O Ephraim, what shall I do to you? O Judah, what shall I do to you? For your faithfulness is like a morning cloud, and like the early dew it goes away" (NKJV).

When I was a teenager I attended church with a young lady who would "pray back through" every summer after school was out. She would attend youth camp and come back all fired up. This state would last until September and the start of another school year. Come September, she would "backslide," not to be seen again until the following June.

There are some people who always seem to "come back" to church every time a revival is held. They will run to the altar, pray in a dramatic fashion, and then quickly disappear shortly after the close of the revival.

One woman who was sharing an apartment with a lesbian lover "came back" during a revival and loudly "prayed back through." She was enthusiastic about coming back to church until the pastor pointed out to her that she needed to leave her current roommate and return to her husband. Her new-found spiritual desire proved to be very short-lived.

It is impossible for a person to continue forever in a double-minded manner. "Doth a fountain send forth at the same place sweet water and bitter? Can the fig tree, my brethren, bear olive berries? either a vine, figs? so can no fountain both yield salt water and fresh" (James 3:11-12).

There comes a time when a person either chooses to live for God, come what may, or chooses rather to turn back to the world. A spiritually unstable individual finds himself in a most miserable condition: he is too worldly for the church and too churchy for the world.

Jesus told us that we would know the true nature of people not by what they say but by the fruit they bear (Matthew 7:15-20). Spiritual instability is eventually fatal to the soul because of the fruit it produces. How foolish it is for someone to spend all his time in pretending to be spiritual and spend none at all in becoming spiritual! Sooner or later his inconsistency will become plain for all to see.

The spiritually unstable person first causes those around him to lose confidence in him. Eventually the unstable person loses confidence in himself. Embarrassment haunts him and drives him more deeply into the world that he had been content to merely flirt with for so long.

Instability evolves into worldliness, and worldliness leads to corruption. The end result is spiritual death—the ugly spiritual death of the backslider.

Next we will examine the role of worldliness in the demise of a backslider.

5

A Heart Divided
by Worldliness

The walls of the lecture hall surrounding the preacher were dazzling in their whiteness. It seemed only seconds ago that he had sadly walked away from the grave of a backslidden young man named Tom. Now the preacher sat in the presence of a tall figure of a man (an angel perhaps?) who was ready to continue his series of lectures concerning Tom's spiritual autopsy. The preacher was beginning to understand, as never before, the factors that contribute to the spiritual demise of a backslider.

"Pastor, it is time to continue our analysis of the anatomy of backslider. So far, we have examined the parts instability, pride, and a lack of knowledge played in the spiritual death of Tom. Today we will examine how worldliness divided Tom's heart, causing him to lose his love for God as his love for the world increased."

Worldliness and godliness are mutually exclusive spiritual characteristics. A worldly individual does not aspire to godliness, just as a godly individual dare not entertain worldliness. The term "worldly Christian" is in fact an oxymoron, for no true Christian is worldly and no worldly individual can truly be described as Christ-like (the literal meaning of the word *Christian*).

Jesus stated emphatically that His followers are not of the world even as He Himself was not of the world (John 17:16). The apostle Paul dealt at length with this principle of separation at length in II Corinthians 6:14-17: "Be ye not unequally yoked together with unbelievers: for what fellowship hath righteousness with unrighteousness? and what communion hath light with darkness? and what concord hath Christ with Belial? or what part hath he that believeth with an infidel? and what agreement hath the temple of God with idols? for ye are the temple of the living God; as God hath said, I will dwell in them, and walk in them; and I will be their God, and they shall be my people. Wherefore come out from among them, and be ye separate, saith the Lord, and touch not the unclean thing; and I will receive you."

From the very beginning God has desired a people separated unto Himself. This is why the Lord established His covenant with Abraham and his descendants. God blessed Israel with the understanding that Israel would destroy the works of the wicked and establish holiness in the earth. But Psalm 106:34-36 describes Israel's embracement of the worldliness God commanded it to destroy. "They did not destroy the peoples, concerning whom the LORD had commanded them, but they mingled with the Gentiles and learned their works; they served their idols, which became a snare to them" (NKJV). Instead of reaching the world, which had been God's plan, Israel allowed the world to reach them. They began adopting the attitudes and habits of the world around them. The mixture of piety and carnality is particularly distasteful to God. In Hosea 7:8 God called Israel a "cake not turned." Such a cake is burnt on one side, and gooey and half-cooked on the other. It is certainly not a sight to stimulate one's appetite. Yet it is the perfect picture of people who try to mix godliness and worldliness.

Today some churches teeter on the brink of repeating Israel's fatal error. Some people feel that they can hold fast to God with one hand and embrace the world with the other.

Strange things happen when God's people mingle with the heathen. For example, it has happened that people with godly hairstyles—men with short hair and women with long, uncut hair—have immodestly put on bathing suits and gone swimming together. Gospel musicians have performed with heavily amplified instruments throbbing to a sensual, hard-rock beat that drowns out the lyrics of the song and with jerking movements that imitate secular rock groups rather than express worship.

Yes, strange things happen when worlds collide. Families sit in church on Sunday and hear that lust, murder, envy, and adultery are sins to be avoided, but on week nights some of these same families sit transfixed in front of television programs that glorify lust, murder, envy, and adultery. Meanwhile, parents who cannot understand the bizarre tastes in clothing and hairstyles of young people need look no further than MTV and other ungodly programming found on TV.

Punk and Pentecost are two mutually exclusive lifestyles. Like light and darkness, these two ways of living can never coexist peacefully, yet some precious Pentecostal youths have sought to emulate the punk lifestyle. Some preachers, who tolerate and even emulate the punk look, have been labeled "New Wave" preachers. These New Wave preachers embrace everything the church stands against. Like Solomon of old, they marry the cultures their fathers fought to overcome.

It has always been the plan of Christ for the church to reach out to the world and seek and save those who are lost. On the other hand, it has always been the design of Satan for the world to infiltrate the church and destroy those who are saved. Satan knows that the strength of the church is its love for God, and thus he tries to redirect the love of the church away from God and toward the world.

The apostle John was very direct in his warning against worldliness: "Do not love the world or the things in the world. If anyone loves the world, the love of the Father is not in him. For all that is in the world—the lust of the flesh, the lust of the eyes, and the pride of life—is not of the Father but is of the world. And the world is passing away, and the lust of it; but he who does the will of God abides forever" (I John 2:15-17, NKJV).

There is no question that the world is placing tremendous pressure on the church. Some Christians make it even more difficult for themselves by bringing the world into their home via the electronic media. In any case, it is essential that the church remain separated from the world. We dare not touch unclean things, we who are to be arrayed in robes of God's righteousness.

Romans 12:2 admonishes us not to be conformed to this world, but to be transformed by the renewing of our minds. We need to be reminded that we are indeed unique. We are not to be like the world around us. We are a "peculiar" (unique) people who have been set apart to demonstrate to the world the saving power of the gospel (I Peter 2:9).

Worldliness will divide our loyalties and sap us of our spiritual strength. If we lose our sense of separation and the concept of holiness we will become even as Samson. Once Samson's hair was cut—a symbol of the breaking of his Nazarite vow of separation—he lost all of his strength. He then became easy prey for an enemy who waited in the wings, eager to blind him once his strength was gone. Likewise, we have an enemy who lies in wait for us, eager to blind us to the truth if we begin to entertain worldliness in our hearts.

When a person is a sinner he is alive to the world and dead to God. Salvation will cause him to die out to the world and come alive to God. Backsliding reverses this process of salvation. If a Christian begins to come alive to the world once more, his relationship with God gradually dies. Godliness gives way to worldliness, and unchecked worldliness brings corruption and idolatry. Thus a worldly heart is always a prominent characteristic of the anatomy of a backslider.

6

Knees Bent the Wrong Way
(Prayerlessness)

" S o far our lectures on the anatomy of a backslider have identified the contributing spiritual factors of worldliness, instability, pride, and a lack of spiritual knowledge. Today we will examine the root of most of these contributing factors, for today we will examine the knee joint of the backslider."

In speaking to Hosea about Israel, the Lord made an interesting statement: "And my people are bent to backsliding from me: though they called them to the most High, none at all would exalt him" (Hosea 11:7). In our first lecture we defined backsliding as a negative response or series of responses to the leading of the Spirit, and we drew a parallel to a cow being led by a farmer. As long as the cow willingly follows the farmer, the farmer has no problem leading the cow. If the cow locks its knees and begins to balk, the farmer will not be able to lead the cow to food, shelter, or anywhere. The backslider has a problem with knees that begin to lock up.

The temptation to resist God's direction is ever present with all of us, due to our fleshly nature. There is only one known prevention for locking knees that are bent to backsliding, and that is keeping the knees flexible by consistently bending them in prayer. Most people started their walk with God by bending their knees in a prayer of repentance. Their knees continued to bend while they sought the Lord for the baptism of the Spirit. The fervor and initial excitement of receiving the Holy Ghost assured that knee bending would continue unabated for a while.

As with honeymooners in the natural realm, it is impossible for new converts' heads to remain in the clouds forever. Sooner or later they must come back to earth and face the task of establishing spiritual discipline, which, after all, is the basis of becoming a disciple.

Knees that are not consistently bent in prayer can become inflexible and eventually become bent instead to backsliding.

Why do sincere, well-meaning people neglect such a vital, life-sustaining function as prayer? People in today's society find it easier to respond to the urgent rather than to the vital. Charles E. Hummel observed this tendency and stated, "The vital task rarely must be done today or even this week. The urgent task calls for instant action. The momentary appeal of these tasks seem irresistible and they devour our energy. But in the light of time's perspective their deceptive prominence fades. With a sense of loss we recall the vital task we pushed aside. We realize we've become slaves to the tyranny of the urgent."

A biblical example of this principle is found in Luke 10:39-42: "And she had a sister called Mary, which also sat at Jesus' feet, and heard his word. But Martha was cumbered about much serving, and came to him, and said, Lord, dost thou not care that my sister hath left me to serve alone? bid her therefore that she help me. And Jesus answered and said unto her, Martha, Martha, thou art careful and troubled about many things: but one thing is needful: and Mary hath chosen that good part, which shall not be taken away from her.''

Many urgent trivialities dominated Martha's thinking. There was food to prepare, tables to be set, and dishes to be cleared. No doubt Mary was also aware of the many duties that clamored for her attention, yet Mary realized that an opportunity to have fellowship with Jesus and learn from Him deserved the highest priority. The dishes would still be there—the work would always be with her—but opportunities for close communion with the Lord were most precious and not to be taken for granted.

Although prayer may not at times seem as urgent to the flesh as other duties, we must remember that nothing is as vital and as life-sustaining to the soul as prayer. How vital is prayer to the spiritual life of an individual? Jesus exhorted Peter on the importance of prayer after Peter had demonstrated his inability to concentrate in prayer for one hour: "Watch and pray, that ye enter not into temptation: the spirit indeed is willing, but the flesh is weak" (Matthew 26:41).

It is interesting to note that there are two meanings of the word *temptation*. First, temptation can mean enticement to do evil. Prayer gives a person spiritual strength to resist the devil and the enticements of the flesh. It enables a person to walk after the Spirit rather than the lusts of the flesh.

Temptation also refers to trials and tests that God

either sends our way or allows to happen. Many times the Lord does so to instruct or correct His children. A person who diligently prays and listens to God may be able to avoid learning lessons the hard way.

Shepherds send out dogs to growl and snap at the sheep who stray from the herd. God sometimes has to send tests and trials to lead strays back into a closer relationship with Him. Who knows the trials we could have been spared from if we had only learned to walk closer to the Lord in prayer?

Jesus let Peter know that a person cannot walk with God on the basis of natural strength. Though in his heart a person may be willing to do what is right, the flesh in itself is weak. The relationship of a human being with God requires supernatural strength that only comes from God through prayer.

Pride, lack of knowledge, instability, and worldliness can all be avoided if consistent prayer exists. Prayer reminds us of God's greatness and helps us maintain humility. Communion with God in prayer stimulates a desire to know Him better and thus creates a hunger for His Word. Prayer helps purge a person of instability. It causes love for God to grow brighter, while love for the world grows ever dimmer.

Unbent knees—knees that are strangers to prayer—usually are a primary contributing cause of spiritual deterioration and an eventual demise. They feature prominently in the anatomy of the backslider.

7

A Tight Fist (The Love of Money)

" " In our previous lectures, we have discussed spiritual factors that contribute to backsliding, including a lack of prayer, a lack of knowledge of God's Word, instability, pride, and worldliness. In considering these factors it is important to realize that a pious individual is not immune to the potential dangers of backsliding. There are spiritual pitfalls even for the person who prays, reads his Bible, is humble, and is stable, and one of the most dangerous of these is a tight fist—a love for money and material possessions."

The apostle Paul warned against attitudes of spiritual complacency. "Wherefore let him that thinketh he standeth take heed lest he fall" (I Corinthians 10:12). The enemy has devised many subtle traps to trip up the unsuspecting Christian. In twentieth-century North America, where materialism and financial success are often worshiped with evangelistic fervor, the most godly of individuals must guard against the love of money supplanting their pure love of God.

Today so much is preached in the media concerning prosperity and God's financial blessings for the believer that one is tempted to think that living a Christian life is an automatic ticket to wealth. Many people judge the degree of God's anointing on a person's life by the size and luxury of the car he drives and the cut and expense of the suit of clothes that he wears. In this environment the inspired advice that Paul gave to Timothy concerning attitudes towards possessions should be taken to heart by every Christian believer: "Men of corrupt minds, and destitute of the truth, supposing that gain is godliness: from such withdraw thyself. But godliness with contentment is great gain. For we brought nothing into this world, and it is certain we can carry nothing out. And having food and raiment let us be therewith content. But they that will be rich fall into temptation and a snare, and into many foolish and hurtful lusts, which drown men in destruction and perdition. For the love of money is the root of all evil: which while some coveted after, they have erred from the faith, and pierced themselves through with many sorrows. But thou, O man of God, flee these things; and follow after righteousness, godliness, faith, love, patience, meekness" (I Timothy 6:5-12).

Every pastor eventually will deal with people who, although they would never dream of committing adultery, lying, killing, or practicing other obvious sins, will let an obsession with money dry up the wells of their souls. People who think nothing of trusting their eternal souls to the teaching of the pastor will question him about every dime the church spends. The thought of the man of God asking for building fund pledges or missions offerings fills this poor fellow with dread. "Doesn't that preacher know that money is hard to come by," he says. "Why, if he keeps up with all these pleas for funds he'll put me and everyone else in the poorhouse." It is sad that some people insist on only the best when it comes to the houses they live in and the cars they drive, yet would be perfectly content if the house of God had to be furnished with a mediocre, bargain-basement decor, especially if it would eliminate the need for special offerings.

The love of money obviously has the ability to drive a wedge between a child of God and his church leadership. A pastor who has a burden for the lost as his top priority is on a collision course with a member whose money and possessions hold the number one position. It is said that one can never really know what makes someone tick until you ask him to share either his time or his money. Jesus taught that wherever a person's treasure is there will his heart be also (Matthew 6:21).

The love of money breeds spiritual discontent, which in turn drives a wedge between a person and God. To see how this is so, let us consider for a moment the following scriptural truths.

First, the joy of the Lord is our strength (Nehemiah 8:10). Without the joy of the Lord in our life, living for God would soon become an unbearable drudgery. Second, in His presence is fullness of joy (Psalm 16:11). We find the joy of the Lord that we need so much when we enter the presence of the Lord.

If the joy of the Lord is truly our strength, and if we find the fullness of joy in the presence of the Lord, then it is vital for us to know how to enter the presence of the Lord. Psalm 100:4 provides instruction about how to enter the presence of the Lord: "Enter into his gates with thanksgiving.'' In order to even get into the front door of God's presence we must approach Him with thanksgiving.

This poses a real problem for the person who has allowed discontent to enter into his life. A love of money and a lust for material gain make it difficult if not impossible for people to be thankful for the things God has blessed them with. No matter what God blesses some people with, it is never quite big enough, new enough, or prestigious enough to suit them. Since the Word teaches us to enter into His gates with thanksgiving, it becomes very hard for discontented individuals to find any comfort in the presence of the Lord. As a result of their lack of thanksgiving, their prayers seem to go nowhere.

Having spent the week grumbling and complaining about all the things in life they have not yet been privileged to obtain, it is not surprising that on Sunday many people have trouble moving into a flow of worship and praise. How can they enter the courts of God with praise if they can't even get past the front gate (thanksgiving)?

The love of money and the discontent that it brings hold other potential perils for the child of God. It almost caused Asaph to backslide and fall away from God: "My feet were almost gone; my steps had well nigh slipped. For I was envious at the foolish, when I saw the prosperity of the wicked. . . . Behold, these are the ungodly, who prosper in the world; they increase in riches. Verily I have cleansed my heart in vain, and washed my hands in innocency" (Psalm 73:2-3, 12-13).

There is a fatal flaw in the philosophy of those who equate godliness with prosperity. Matthew 5:45 says that God sends rain on both the just and the unjust. Prosperity does not always come in direct proportion to faith and godliness. Among the ranks of the prosperous, there are some godly folks but also some of the most wretched and wicked people on earth today. Yes, some people never tithe, go to church, or give to missions, and yet are swimming in prosperity. On the other hand many godly men and women will never be in a *Who's Who of Millionaires*.

Although David declared that he had never seen the righteous forsaken nor his seed begging bread, he never said that the righteous and his seed would wear the most expensive clothing available and would travel in stretch limousines. The promise to those who seek first the kingdom of God and His righteousness is that God will supply their needs. Our needs are food, clothing, and adequate shelter. For example, most of earth's population will never own an automobile of their own, but in North America some Christians complain if their car is not as nice as the person's next door. Some overfed Christians in North America go to church feeling so sorry for themselves that they can hardly worship, while thousands elsewhere go to bed hungry every night.

How often do people thank God for food to eat and clothes to wear? Yet how many times do people complain because they cannot afford steak but have to eat hamburger, and because they are tired of wearing the same old suit, dress, or shoes?

Godliness with contentment is great gain. Blessed is the person unfettered by the tyranny of unrequited materialism. No one can serve two masters. Either Jesus is Lord of our lives or the "almighty dollar" is. When the church tries to motivate some people to share the good news of salvation with a friend or neighbor, their eyes glaze over with apathy and unconcern. But when the same people hear that they can strike it rich by selling soap, vitamins, or snake oil to a friend or a neighbor, they will display unfettered enthusiasm.

Is there then some special spiritual quality in being impoverished? Does the Bible encourage people to renounce all ambition and drive? Not at all! The poverty that is a result of sloth and laziness gives no glory to God but rather reproaches the sluggard. God intends for a person to work, and there are financial rewards for the person who is not afraid to apply himself faithfully to his labors.

The key is to establish the proper priorities in our life. Whether we believe it or not, there are more important things in life than money.

First, our relationship with God and the salvation of our soul are far more important than the amount of wealth that we can accumulate. A person who constantly misses church to swing a financial deal or to earn a lot of overtime needs to reexamine his priorities. A person who places luxuries over his giving to God needs to consider his spiritual responsibilities prayerfully.

Second, the welfare of our families is more important than possessions we may acquire. Many a man has worked overly long hours in order to afford luxuries, only to discover that he is a stranger to his children. Such men never seem to realize that children need the presence and guidance of a father more than they need possessions. Only time will reveal the tragic results of mothers who forsook their God-given role of raising their small children just to earn a few dollars in the marketplace so they could enjoy a high standard of living. Many children grow up without Mom's loving touch because Mom and Dad preferred possessions over the welfare of their children. It is one thing for Mom to work because of necessity; it is another thing altogether to sacrifice children on the altar of materialism.

Finally, contentment and peace of mind are more important than any goods we could acquire. The person who has great gain is the person who has not only acquired godliness but also contentment as well.

Upon examining the anatomy of a backslider, it is not uncommon to find that along with the other problems such as an empty head, locked knee joints, and a divided heart, many times he suffered from a tight fist that held much too tightly to the riches of this world.

8

In Summary

The lecturer strode to the podium and looked out at the sad countenance of the preacher. "Pastor, I know that observing the spiritual autopsy of your former saint, Tom, has been a painful experience. Today you will hear the conclusion of the matter. You have received a detailed explanation concerning the anatomy of a backslider. Soon you will be returned to earth and your flock. There you can convey these truths to your church."

The pastor sighed and leaned back in his chair. "If I can keep just one individual from ending up a spiritual casualty like Tom, I will be most happy." Leaning forward intently he added, "I know this: I hate sin and what it does to people. I hate even the very word *backslider.*"

"Very few people can comprehend the burden a pastor carries for his people," the lecturer said. "Nor can they know how backsliders break the heart of both men and God.

"Our last six lectures identified the following major flaws in the anatomy of a backslider:

1. An empty head indicated a lack of spiritual knowledge.
2. An upturned nose revealed a life full of pride.
3. A mouth that spoke from both sides exhibited instability.
4. Close examination of the heart revealed a marked division caused by worldliness.
5. The knee joints were stiff and locked, portraying a life devoid of prayer.
6. A tight fist displayed the love of money that contributed to the spiritual demise of the backslider.

"Our autopsy revealed two other items as well. Upon backsliding, the feet began once more to walk in the paths of sin. Sadly, these same feet had one time walked in the paths of righteousness. The hands that had for so long been lifted in prayer and praise were given over once more to corruption. Lust conceived and brought forth sin; sin in turn gave birth to death. Today, we want to conclude our lecture series by briefly surveying other influences that are sometimes part of a backslider's anatomy."

One such problem is an eye fixed on evil things. Paul warned the Corinthians church about lusting after evil things and used the history of Israel as an example: "But with many of them God was not well pleased: for they were overthrown in the wilderness. Now these things were our examples to the intent we should not lust after evil things, as they also lusted" (I Corinthians 10:5-6).

There are many things that otherwise good Christians can find themselves lusting for. Some lust for the wrong crowd. Young people especially are vulnerable in this area. They desire to associate with the wrong people and to win their approval. But we are judged by the company we keep, and more importantly, we are profoundly influenced by the company we keep. In particular, II Corinthians 6:14 warns us not to be unequally yoked with unbelievers. Therefore, Christian young people should not waste their time and risk their souls by dating sinners. They should not merely look for physical beauty, but search for a companion who truly loves and obeys the Lord.

Some people lust for the wrong kinds of music, literature, and entertainment. We are not to love the world or the things that are in the world. The violence, illicit sex, and occult themes that permeate much of this world's entertainment are offensive to God and grieve the Holy Spirit of promise, by whom we are sealed. (See Ephesians 4:30.)

Many homes have been broken and lives devastated because men and women allowed themselves to lust for a partner other than their spouse. No matter how much the world may glamorize adultery, it is still a sin that results in tragic consequences.

It is a dangerous thing to lust after evil things. Our eyes should be firmly fixed upon Jesus.

Another influence that can cause an individual to stray from God is a false gospel. Paul wrote to the Galatians, "I marvel that ye are so soon removed from him that called you into the grace of Christ unto another gospel: which is not another; but there be some that trouble you, and would pervert the gospel of Christ" (Galatians 1:6-7). We live in a world that is witnessing an explosion of religion. Television and radio offer a veritable smorgasbord of religious broadcasting in which voices and doctrines of all kinds can be heard. People with itching ears follow false teachers who send out messages tailor-made to attract followers and finances.

In this environment, we must not only guard ourselves morally, but we also need to keep ourselves doctrinally pure. Paul admonished Timothy, "Take heed unto thyself, and unto the doctrine; continue in them: for in doing this thou shalt both save thyself, and them that hear thee" (I Timothy 4:16).

A person who listens to every Reverend Tom, Dick, and Harry of the airwaves only invites doctrinal confusion into his life. We must choose our spiritual diet carefully. Before a person becomes caught up in listening to or following after an ecclesiastical superstar he should counsel with his pastor. The local pastor is the God-ordained shepherd, and he can provide direction to pure sources of spiritual refreshment. Even ministers need to carefully examine and screen in light of Scripture what they read and hear from popular and "successful" religious sources.

False teachers have poisoned the minds and hearts of many a gullible Christian, causing confusion, heartache, and even spiritual destruction. Saints should beware of any preacher who is eager to entice them through flattery and other means into forsaking their pastor and brothers and sisters in the local church.

Finally, we must avoid the double-edged sword of Satan that has caused many to fall away and fail: the sword of tribulation and prosperity. It has been said that every Christian goes through the tests of poverty and prosperity.

Jesus taught His disciples about people who would believe the Word but falter when the going got tough:

"The same is he that heareth the word, and anon with joy receiveth it; yet hath he not root in himself, but dureth for a while: for when tribulation or persecution ariseth because of the word, by and by he is offended" (Matthew 13:20-21). There are some whose faith in God evaporates at the first hint of trouble. Unless the bills are all paid and all systems are go, they cannot maintain an attitude of thanksgiving and praise. The first test of their faith sends them careening out of the church back into sin.

On the other hand, there are those who come through trials of tribulation, persecution, and deprivation unscathed and full of victory. They pass the poverty test with flying colors. The harder things become, the more they trust God. Then they face the other edge of the devil's sword: the test of prosperity. "Beware that thou forget not the LORD thy God . . . lest when thou hast eaten and art full, and hast built goodly houses, and dwelt therein; and when thy herds and thy flocks multiply, and thy silver and thy gold is multiplied, and all that thou hast is multiplied; then thine heart be lifted up, and thou forget the LORD thy God" (Deuteronomy 8:11-14).

If poverty and trouble have killed their thousands, prosperity has killed its tens of thousands. But the Lord intends for His people to serve Him faithfully, regardless of circumstances. (See Philippians 4:11-13.)

"Pastor, it is obvious that the anatomy of a backslider is an inexhaustible subject. Many are the reasons and excuses that people use to forsake their Savior. I hope that I have shown you enough to help you prevent others from casting away their hope in Christ. It is time for you to return to your labors.

"By the way, Pastor, let me say one more thing.

There will be those who will try to blame you or others for their failure. Preach the Word, teach, exhort, do your best to restore those who have fallen—but do not blame yourself or accept blame from others. In the end, each person must work out his own salvation in fear and trembling. Nothing external can separate a man from the love of God. A person who backslides chooses the path he takes and will answer to God alone. Go and preach."

● ● ● ●

The voice of the preacher's wife startled him to awareness as if he were awakening from a long sleep. "Honey, you preached the best funeral message that you could, especially when you consider the circumstances."

The preacher's hand gripped the steering wheel of his car. He had returned to the exact moment of time when he had been snatched away to the lecture hall. He still felt the sorrow and regret of watching a former saint die lost and without God, yet mixed with those feelings was an exhilaration of purpose.

His wife briefly hugged him, and wanting to change the subject, she asked, "What are you teaching tomorrow night at Bible study?"

"I believe I am going to begin a series of studies that I'll call 'The Anatomy of a Backslider.'" He smiled, placed the car in gear, and drove toward the church with more determination than he had felt in years.